10 0346881 X

D1428489

UNIVERSITY OF NOTTINGHAM

SWAN

SA

D

INFORMATION

2 9 MAY 2007

POTTERY
IN ROMAN BRITAIN

Fourth edition
(substantially rewritten and with completely new figures)

SHIRE ARCHAEOLOGY

2

Cover illustration
A New Forest colour-coated bottle-like flask decorated with painted patterns in white overslip, edged with bands of rouletting (*c.*250/60—320). The variable colouring of the surface is the result of the firing sequence and stacking arrangements within the kiln. The flask was probably stacked upside down in the kiln-oven with its base and upper part inside other vessels (perhaps in beakers). The kiln load was probably first fired with a free supply of oxygen, making the whole exterior coating of the flask turn a red-orange colour *(oxidised)*. Towards the end of the firing the kiln was apparently clamped down to exclude oxygen and produce a smoke-laden *(reducing)* atmosphere. This changed the exposed central part of the exterior of the pot to a dark brown. The upper and lower parts of the flask, however, were protected as a result of being stacked inside other vessels; they thus failed to come into contact with the reducing atmosphere, or were not exposed to it long enough to change their surface colour. In these areas the flask remained oxidised and red-orange.
(Photograph: K. Grinstead.)

In memoriam
J.P.G.

2

British Library Cataloguing in Publication Data available

Published by
SHIRE PUBLICATIONS LTD
Cromwell House, Church Street, Princes Risborough,
Aylesbury, Bucks HP17 9AJ, UK.

Series Editor: James Dyer

Copyright © Vivien G. Swan, 1975, 1978, 1980 and 1988.
All rights reserved.
No part of this publication may be reproduced or transmitted in any form or by any means, electronic or mechanical, including photocopy, recording, or any information storage and retrieval system, without permission in writing from the publishers.

ISBN 0 85263 912 0

First published 1975
Second edition 1978
Third edition 1980
Fourth edition 1988

Set in 11 point Times and printed in Great Britain by
C. I. Thomas & Sons (Haverfordwest) Ltd,
Press Buildings, Merlins Bridge, Haverfordwest, Dyfed.

Contents

4

List of illustrations

1003468881X

Preface to the fourth edition

This book is intended as an outline to the pottery forms and fabrics most widely distributed in Roman Britain, and the development of major production centres. Specialist terms (such as may be found on museum labels or excavation reports) which are not explained in the text or by illustations will be found in the glossary. All dates are AD unless otherwise stated. Centuries are indicated by simple Roman numerals alone. In common with standard practice, pottery has been drawn with the external elevation on the right and a thickness section on the left (as if a quadrant had been cut away). Thus, external decoration appears on the right of the dividing line and internal features on the left. Brackets indicate restored sections of vessels, in every case based on the evidence of more complete comparable specimens.

Since the appearance of the first edition of this book there has been an upsurge of research and publication on the subject, which has thrown much new light on material included in previous editions and that which was scarcely recognised then. In this fourth edition, the text has been substantially rewritten and entirely new figures drawn to incorporate some of this new information. To avoid confusion in the quoting of numbers of vessel-types from previous editions, the new vessel numbering in the figures here starts at 101.

I would like to acknowledge assistance from the following: C. Johns and V. Rigby (British Museum), B. Blake (Derby Museum), P. Sealey (Colchester and Essex Museum), Salisbury Museum, and my colleagues Philip Sinton and Stephanie Harding (Royal Commission on the Historical Monuments of England). Thanks are due to Derby Museum, Oxford Archaeological Excavation Committee, the Rheinisches Landesmuseum, Trier, the Royal Commission on the Historical Monuments of England, A. Selkirk *(Current Archaeology),* and the Trustees of the British Museum, for permission to reproduce photographs; to Ken Grinstead for the cover illustration and plates 21-3 and 27; and to Nick Griffiths for drawing the kiln reconstruction (plate 28). Above all, I owe much to the work of my colleagues in the Study Group for Roman Pottery, particularly to Kay Hartley for help on mortaria, to Graham Webster, who first fostered my interest in Romano-British pottery, and last but not least to John Gillam for his unstinting kindness, encouragement and friendship over fifteen years. It is to his memory that this new edition is dedicated.

Glossary

Barbotine: relief decoration executed by trailing semi-liquid clay squeezed through the end of some implement on to a finished vessel before firing, a process identical to icing a cake (plates 1, 7, 16 and 17).

Bead-rim: a rim swelling outwards into a simple rounded shape (plates 5 and 23; figure V, 42; figure IX, 171).

Burnishing: a smooth (sometimes shiny) area of a pot obtained by the pressure or rubbing action of a tool applied immediately before firing.

Carination: a sharp inward change of angle in the body of a vessel.

Colour-coat: See *slip*.

Cornice rim: a rim projecting outwards and decoratively moulded (as in an architectural cornice): plates 16-17; figure IV, 139-40.

Everted rim: a rim turning sharply outwards and upwards from the wall of the vessel; often curved (plate 2; figure IV, 138; figure V, 144, 146).

Fabric or **paste:** the prepared clay with which a vessel was manufactured.

Foot-ring: a low raised ring added to the base of the vessel to aid stability (plates 3, 4; figure V, 145; figure XII, 199, 201-2, 204-6).

Gallo-Belgic: the latest iron age culture of Gaul before the Roman conquest and (here) the pottery whose style was influenced by it.

Paint: see *slip*.

Rough-cast decoration: for technique see chapter 4 and figure IV, 139-40.

Rouletting: incised decoration made by a toothed wheel or roller applied while the vessel was turning on the potter's wheel (plate 10).

Rusticated decoration: for technique see chapter 2 and plate 14.

Slip, colour-coat, paint: The term *slip* refers to both a solution of clay and water (with or without added colorants) into which a vessel could be dipped, and the resultant finish after firing. When such a slip is made darker (by means of added minerals) than the paste of the vessel which it covers it is often called a *colour-coat*. The term *paint* is used in the sense of a thick slip (white or coloured) applied decoratively (by brush or other implement) to the finished surface of a pot before firing (plate 10).

Temper: small mineral or vegetable particles, for example sand, crushed shell, potsherds *(grog),* limestone, flint, charcoal or grass, which are mixed with the clay paste of a vessel at manufacture to reduce plasticity and prevent too much shrinkage on firing.

Wall-sided: used of a vessel whose side rises vertically above a carination and terminates in a plainish rim; a feature of certain mortaria (figure X, 187).

1
Introduction

Pottery is undoubtedly the commonest archaeological material surviving on Roman sites, and its study is important for three main reasons: firstly, as a chronological indicator when other datable objects such as coins are lacking; secondly, for the information it can provide on trade, communications and social development when examined distributionally; and thirdly, as a tool in understanding the history of ceramic technology.

When the Roman army invaded Britain in 43 they found a number of potting traditions already established. On the one hand the wealthy communities of the South-east and parts of southern and eastern England, who already had close links with the continent, were importing quality tablewares and mass-producing and trading wheel-thrown pottery on a considerable scale. On the other hand, elsewhere pottery was handmade, with a few notable exceptions, mostly on a fairly small scale for relatively local markets; further research, however, may indicate more long-distance trade in such handmade wares. There were even parts of Britain where the iron age inhabitants do not seem to have made pottery *(aceramic)*, but must have used wood or leather only. The Romans were adaptable; so while many alien types of vessel, such as flagons and mortaria, were widely introduced in quantity for the first time at the conquest, some native British iron age forms, such as the handled mug or tankard, were soon assimilated and spread.

Initially, therefore, the invading army had to import some of its pottery and immediately encourage native craftsmen to cater for it. The fort at Waddon Hill, Dorset, for instance, acquired as much as 80 per cent of its pottery locally. Evidence also suggests that Gallic, Danubian and other continental potters came over in the army, or in the army's wake, to take advantage of the situation, for example at Chichester, West Sussex, and Usk, Gwent. Similarly, entrepreneurs would have arrived, ready to locate and expand suitable potteries with an eye on obtaining orders to supply the Roman army. Such a deal was one of the most decisive factors for the development of any manufacturing centre. It could raise a workshop from being a supplier of purely local status to a long-distance exporter of pre-eminent industrial rank. Although no contract documents relating to pottery survive for anywhere in the Roman Empire, it is clear, from the combined local and non-local distributions of many specialist products, that such agreements, direct or indirect, must have existed.

As a last resort, in the earlier phases of campaigning, in hostile aceramic regions, where supplies were unobtainable locally or at risk from ambush, the legions or auxiliaries seem to have undertaken or directly supervised pottery manufacture themselves. Sometimes, as at Brampton, Cumbria, this was carried out jointly with tile production. In late I and early II such supply depots were the norm in frontier zones, but about 120 most closed down in a reorganisation of supply procedures. This left the garrisons dependent on pottery transported from civilian factories further south. More rarely, as apparently at York, the former military industry passed into civilian ownership and continued in production.

At first the major industries were primarily concerned with supplying specialist vessels, such as mortaria, flagons and tablewares, to the Roman army (sometimes from considerable distances) and to the developing new towns. As romanisation and prosperity spread, so the countryside began to purchase romanised vessels in quantity. Thus, by late II, a number of major specialist industries in the Midlands and South prospered on civilian demand alone, and imports had declined drastically. In addition, numerous smaller potteries of comparatively local significance flourished and were the main suppliers of the civil markets. Some, originally set up to supply local garrisons, had declined in importance and narrowed their output when the troops moved north. Ultimately most major settlements would have had kilns nearby or been supplied by peripatetic craftsmen operating on a cyclical basis at various locations within the adjacent region. Such local products, mainly kitchen wares, were often influenced by native iron age traditions and many items continued to be handmade or partly handmade throughout the Roman period. These workshops manufactured perhaps between 70 and 80 per cent of all the pottery in Roman Britain, and except in Wales and the North-west (where no indigenous potting traditions existed) most probably never traded their wares more than 10 to 15 miles (16 to 24 km). This helps to explain the great diversity of wares from region to region.

Methods of dating pottery are varied and often complex. When vessels are found in archaeological deposits which are linked to historical events mentioned by contemporary Roman authors, we may infer that they were in current use then. For instance, excavations in the towns of Colchester, London and Verulamium (St Albans) have revealed burnt layers resulting from the Boudican rebellion of 61. Vessels sometimes occur in deposits dated by inscriptions or large numbers of associated coins. Relatively securely linked to such a chronology is the material from several phases of occupation on the northern frontiers, particularly Hadrian's and the Antonine walls. For these, contemporary historical sources exist and inscriptions are more numerous. Since most wares found there were supplied from factories further south, the northern dates are often transferred to identical products circulating in other parts of Britain. An understanding of northern frontier chronologies is essential for anyone studying Romano-British pottery.

When such evidence is lacking archaeologists sometimes resort to *typology*. Fashions in the shapes, fabrics and decoration of Roman pots changed in the course of time. Thus vessels of the same general type, but each exhibiting minor differences in detail, may be arranged in a sequence showing their development in time (called a *type series*). This method has drawbacks, as rates and even directions of evolution or devolution are often unknown, and the resultant time scale is only relative.

Other chronological problems are posed by archaeological deposits containing pots which were already antiques *(survivals)* when discarded, or coins which had circulated for many decades before their deposition. On sites intensively occupied for several centuries (particularly towns), the rebuilding of structures often caused earlier layers to be disturbed and their ceramic content to be reburied alongside later material. Such pottery (termed *residual* or *rubbish survival*) cannot always be readily separated except when occasionally, like long-circulating coins, it appears worn and abraded or is clearly incompatible with its associations.

In general, imported pottery (particularly samian and other fine wares) and the more specialised, widely marketed British products are more closely datable than vessels with purely local distributions. The excavations of major kiln sites often enables dates assigned to their more widely traded products to be transferred to locally distributed ranges found in the same kiln deposit. Kiln sites also yield valuable information on the sources of wares not otherwise assignable and aid the understanding of distribution patterns, marketing and pottery-manufacturing techniques.

The pottery types, fashions and production centres discussed below (except mortaria and regional wares) have been dealt with in chronological order of their first appearance. Some, however, survived much longer than others and overlap later introductions. Other products underwent more rapid change and tend therefore to be more valuable for dating. The whole subject is undoubtedly more complex than set out here, but more detail can be pursued by means of the booklist and from the substantial bibliographies within some of the publications listed.

Samian ware, a massive subject on its own, has been dealt with relatively briefly here as it is the subject of another book in the Shire Archaeology series and several other general introductions are available.

2
AD *c.*43 to 120

In the period immediately after the invasion the importation of tablewares and other classical vessels, already established in parts of Britain for almost a century, increased in volume. At the same time many new imports arrived. These and much of the commercial production in the southern part of the new province (particularly of specialist vessels) were at first geared to the requirements of Roman garrisons and new administrative centres. From mid I, and particularly after 70 as the army moved northwards, the rapid growth of towns on the sites of former forts in the Midlands and South provided nuclei of romanised people. These required not only basic kitchen wares, but also the ranges of specialist vessels whose traditional use had already been established by the troops. The locations of the first important Romano-British potteries were thus often at urban centres, or near roads or the sea, for good long-distance access to army consumers. From the end of I, when it became clear that Wales and the North were garrisoned on a permanent basis, there was a tendency for prominent specialist producers to move northwards nearer their military markets. For example, by 150 the important early mortarium industry near Verulamium had declined and the Midland workshops at Mancetter/Hartshill (some founded by immigrants from the former) had replaced it in importance.

Gallo-Belgic wares from the Reims area, Trier (Moselle) and other centres were already being shipped into South-east England and beyond from *c.*15/10 BC and may have been manufactured in Hertfordshire and Essex before AD 40, processes greatly stimulated by the Roman military conquest. This resulted in a distribution concentrated mainly south and east of a line from the Humber to the Solent. These standardised ranges of fine polished cups and platters with a *foot-ring* (figure I, 105-8) and beakers and pedestalled cups were made in *terra rubra (TR:* pale fabrics with an orange-red *slip* or orange fabrics without a slip) and *terra nigra (TN:* pale grey to black pastes). Some were impressed with the potter's stamp or trademark. The dominant beaker-forms comprised the concave-sided *girth-beaker* and the commoner barrel-shaped *butt-beaker* (made in terra rubra and fine whitish fabrics, and widely imitated); rouletting within horizontal grooving featured recurrently on both (figure I, 103-4). *Egg-shell terra* *nigra,* extremely thin-walled vessels, such as biconical beakers (some with barbotine dots), was a post-conquest arrival (figure I, 109-10); for *micaceous TR* see mica-dusted wares, below.

Until AD 40 terra rubra was the dominant Gallo-Belgic ware in Britain, but its importation waned to extinction in 65 as a result of competition from the increasing importation of samian ware, which was also orange, and from terra nigra produced more cheaply in the newly established British workshops. In the South-east samian was outnumbered by Gallo-Belgic imports until 50, but the position was radically reversed thereafter. Terra nigra continued to be made until *c*.80 (figure I, 108), and coarser imitations until early II.

Samian ware or **terra sigillata.** This distinctive, glossy, red-coated, mass-produced tableware, often relief-decorated, was reaching South and South-east Britain from the end of the first century BC, but after AD 43 it arrived in greater volume as army supply, and by 55/60 it was flooding into the province. Except for small quantities of pre-conquest wares from Arezzo and allied Italian workshops, imports to Britain were manufactured mainly in South Gaul, in centres such as La Graufesenque, France, until *c*.110. The Central Gaulish factories, notably Lezoux, near Clermont Ferrand, then took over as the main source to Britain. By the end of II these too had ceased trading with Britain. Thereafter lesser amounts of samian arrived from a few smaller East Gaulish workshops until mid III, when the traffic ceased.

A range of cups, bowls (plate 7), platters, jars, mortaria and even inkwells is known. Both plain and decorated vessels often bear the name-stamp of the potters or firms (plate 5) and may be fairly closely dated. Most decorated samian vessels were made in moulds (plate 6), impressed with stamps of mythological figures, animals, birds, scenes from everyday life, and foliage trails; thus it is often possible to assign a vessel to a particular potter from the style or decorative details. Rouletting, barbotine and incised 'cut-glass' style decoration and 'marbled' and black-coated vessels *(black samian,* chapter 4) also occur. The numerous standardised vessel-forms have been given numbers for easy identification, mostly by an archaeologist named Dragendorff (abbreviated to Drag or Dr).

As the main factories declined, numerous smaller centres emerged over the Roman Empire producing copies of samian and divergent forms, sometimes *colour-coated:* for example, *Colchester samian* (a short-lived ware, locally distributed in mid II),

African red slip ware (below), *Argonne ware* (chapter 5), and the various British varieties of *late imitation samian* (chapter 5).

Early imitation of samian. The popularity of samian was such that in late I and early/mid II several workshops in eastern England began to produce imitations of samian (and Gallo-Belgic) bowl and cup forms, often in fine grey-black fabrics in a terra nigra tradition, with a polished surface, decorated with rouletting, comb-incised lines, compass-scribed circles or impressed stamps. Once termed *London ware,* they are now known to have also been made at Wattisfield and West Stow in Suffolk, Ardleigh (Essex), Upchurch (Kent; plate 8) and at unlocated centres in the Nene Valley (Northamptonshire/Cambridgeshire) and the Waveney Valley (Norfolk/Suffolk; figure V, 144-5). Their floruit, at the end of I and in early II, coincided with a temporary shortage of samian.

Orange ware vessels also imitating samian forms, but generally plainer and in traditions arriving with the army, were manufactured in mid/late I to early II at centres such as Usk (Gwent), Wroxeter (Shropshire) and the Gloucester area (figure II, 117-19), Holt (Clwyd), York (*Eburacum ware*) and Caerleon (Gwent; *Caerleon ware*), largely for military markets.

Mica-dusted or mica-gilt ware. The technique of coating tablewares with a slip containing innumerable particles of mica to give a bronze or gold finish (termed mica-dusting) was fashionable in the north-western provinces of the late republic and early empire. Earliest imports to south-eastern Britain included reddish-brown lid-seated jars (*c.*20 BC to AD 10) and fine cream butt-like jars with barbotine ridges and chevrons (AD *c.*10-50), both from Central Gaul (figure I, 101-2). They were painted with a band of mica-wash on the rim and shoulder only. Platters in a *micaceous TR* fabric emanated from the same area (10 BC to AD 25).

From the conquest until *c.*80/90, globular beakers, probably from Gallo-Belgic industries in the Rhineland or Gallia Belgica (perhaps near Braives), were prized, particularly by the troops. They had an overall mica-dusted finish and decoration often of raised bosses or cordons (plate 2; figure IV, 136).

In late I and early II, and occasionally earlier, perhaps partly in response to a samian shortage, British workshops made mica-gilt vessels. These often copied continental tableware forms, particularly deep flanged bowls (figure IV, 137), indented beakers, Gallo-Belgic dishes and bronze jugs. Production is attested at

Gloucester, London, Canterbury and Staines. The fashion had declined by mid II, but a little was made at Colchester and allied East Anglian workshops in mid/late II to early III (figure X, 180).

Amphorae, large two-handled containers used as trade packaging for certain perishables in the Mediterranean world, had been imported to South and South-east Britain in small numbers from the early first century BC and greatly increased at the conquest. Common forms (first classified by an epigrapher, Dressel) included a globular variety containing olive oil from South Spain (Dressel 20). Another type (Dressel 2-4), with a long cylindrical neck, angular handles and a narrow body tapering to a short spike, held wine mainly from Italy and Spain. Wine and figs from Rhodes and the Aegean were shipped in a similar form with peaked handles, the so-called *'Rhodian type'* (plate 24). Fish sauce *(garum)* from Baetica (South Spain) arrived in a range of spiked torpedo-shaped vessels (Dressel 7-11). Apart from the Italian spindle-shaped wine amphorae of the first century BC (Dressel 1), most examples in Britain date from early I to late II AD, but a few rilled wine containers from North Africa arrived in IV and V. Amphorae sometimes bear the name-stamp of the producer, or painted inscriptions indicating date, source and contents. They were reused to pack a wide variety of foodstuffs. British manufacture of amphorae is known only at Staines, Surrey (Dressel 30), and Brockley Hill, Greater London (Dressel 3-4 and possibly 30), where it was linked to mortarium production in late I to early II (chapter 3).

The flagon, a narrow-mouthed, single- or double-handled globular vessel, was used for serving wine. Although small quantities from Central Gaul had reached South and South-east Britain from the end of the first century BC, it was the army of conquest which established its widespread use, at first either importing or stimulating the first British production (often alongside that of mortaria, chapter 3). One universal characteristic of I and II was a light-coloured fabric. If available clays fired too dark, flagon manufacturers coated them with a pale slip. In III and IV flagons became generally smaller and more bottle-like, perhaps indicative of slightly different usage.

    Hofheim-type flagons (figure II, 111), shipped in from Gaul from *c.*10 BC, or made in Britain from AD *c.*43-70 (for example, at Hoo, Kent, or Colchester), were popular with the military. They had almost cylindrical necks, out-curved lips (basically triangular in section) and squared handles. The name Hofheim comes from a well known military site of mid I in Holland where varieties of the form were first clearly defined and published early in the twentieth century.

Ring-necked flagons. This most common type, introduced by the army, had a mouthpiece of multiple superimposed rings. In mid I the neck-top was more or less vertical (figure II, 112), but the rings soon began to splay outwards. During II the top ring thickened and protruded, sometimes becoming internally cupped, while the lower rings became fewer (figure X, 181) or even degenerated into mere grooving; the square handles of I also developed a more rounded profile and foot-rings became shallower.

Flanged-neck flagons. A wide variety, usually with very narrow necks, was current in III and IV. Products of the major centres were often colour-coated and sometimes decorated with rouletting or painted motifs (plate 22; figure XII, 200).

Face-neck flagons, in which the neck terminated in a moulded, sometimes painted and often elaborately coiffed female head, were produced in late III and IV by several fineware industries, such as Crambeck (plate 25), Hadham (figure XIV, 216), Swanpool (figure XIII, 212) and Oxford.

Other common first-century and early second-century vessel-types. Only a selection of the many introduced at the conquest, or developed shortly after and widely manufactured, has been discussed, but more can be found on figure III. A considerable number of them were introduced by the army of conquest and are similar to types found in the Rhenish and Danubian provinces, whence some of the units were drawn. Many exotic forms died out after 120, when most of the military depots closed down.

Carinated bowls (figure IV, 134) with a flat or grooved *(reeded)* rim were initially introduced by the army, which encouraged local production. They terminated *c.*150 in the south, but a little earlier in the north, probably as a result of the influx of black-burnished ware bowls, whose early forms they clearly influenced (figure VIII, 164).

Poppy-head beakers (plate 9). Shaped like poppy seed-heads, with panels or lozenges of raised dots over a grey or black polished fabric, these emerged in *c.*60/70 in south-eastern Britain from Middle Rhineland antecedents but were not common until II. Their sources included Highgate Wood, London *(c.*85/100-160), and, from *c.*70 to early/mid III, the Medway estuary, whence they were shipped to the northern frontiers, mainly between *c*.120 and 190. An overall tendency was for the profile to become ovoid and proportionately taller; by late II/early III the rim was splayed out beyond the girth and the decoration either absent or of simple rouletted bands.

Rustic or rusticated ware (plate 14) was a fashion normally associated with grey jars (probably for cooking), in which a very thick slip, applied after the vessels were thrown, was worked up with the fingers into rough knobs, parallel ridges or spidery encrustations. A continental form popular with the army, it was made in England between 50 and 120. After 70 production and distribution tended to be geared to the northern garrisons, until it was superseded there in the 120s by the influx of black-burnished cooking-pots (chapter 4). Elsewhere it rarely outlasted mid II.

Icenian rusticated ware, unrelated in origin, and locally distributed from potteries in Norfolk and north Suffolk in late II to late III, was characterised by grey cooking-pots with a band of simple diagonal rustication on the shoulder, sometimes combined with slashing (figure XVIII, 248).

Colour-coated wares, fine table vessels with a *slip-coating* darker than the *fabric* from which they were made, varied throughout the Roman period in shape, colour and decoration, depending on their date and source of manufacture.

Pre-Flavian colour-coated wares, small, thin-walled, hemispherical cups and globular beakers, formerly known as 'varnished ware', were imported from 43 to *c*.75 (mainly for the army) from several continental sources, such as Baetica, South Spain (plate 1), and particularly near Lyon, France *(Lyon ware)*. The latter had a pale greenish-cream fabric, with a glossy brown slip and decoration in the form of applied scales (plate 1), roundels with raspberry-like impressions (figure II, 114), *rustication* (plate 1) or sand *rough-casting* (figure II, 115). Rare on non-military sites in Britain, these were sometimes copied in mid I, for example at Eccles, Kent (figure II, 116), and at Colchester for military veterans in the new colonial town.

Central Gaulish colour-coated wares from Lezoux (Clermont Ferrand), scarce among imports of mid I, substantially increased their share of the market between *c*.60/70 and *c*.120. Globular beakers predominated, with a sharply pointed rim, a hard white non-micaceous paste, a thin black, often lustrous slip, and barbotine 'hair-pin and tear-drop' decoration (figure IV, 138) or pelleted clay rough-casting immediately below the rim. For other colour-coated wares imported from late I, see chapter 4.

Lead-glazed wares, also introduced with the army, came from several production centres in the Allier Valley, Central Gaul (including St Rémy en Rollat and Vichy), from 43 to late I. These thin-walled tablewares comprised flagons, bowls and cups with moulded or applied relief decoration (plate 3), and cups and beakers with barbotine dots, loops or scales, all in a white paste with a yellow to green or brown vitreous surface.

Romano-British lead-glazed tablewares, never common, were usually orange or grey in fabric. They were mostly manufactured in late I to early II, occasionally for the army, as at Little Chester (Derby), Holt (Clwyd) and Caerleon (Gwent), but also in civilian contexts, as at Chichester (West Sussex) and near Staines (Surrey). Globular beakers, flagons, and bowls imitating samian forms were generally popular, with barbotine or incised decoration overglazed in brown or green to give contrasting tones (plate 4).

Egg-shell wares, vessels with extremely thin walls, had a long tradition in the Roman world. The earliest in Britain comprised North Italian colour-coated ware, mainly small cups in a red-brown fabric with dark grey-black surfaces, imported in small quantities between *c.*43 and 70 (figure II, 113). In late I and early II small-scale production of egg-shell wares is attested in the London area (conical beakers of eastern affinities, and small hemispherical and segmental bowls in a white fabric with a buffish surface), at Holt (Clwyd) and possibly Caerleon (Gwent). For *egg-shell terra nigra* see Gallo-Belgic wares, chapter 2.

Pompeian red ware (figure III, 129-130), shallow flat-bottomed lidded dishes, with a thick, bright red internal slip, which were used for baking flat bread, were ubiquitous in the Roman Empire from the first century BC. From early in the first century AD, and particularly from mid to late I, small quantities reached Britain from various sources including the vicinity of Pompeii, Italy (probably pre-79), the Auvergne, Central France (increasingly after 79), West Flanders, and perhaps the Eastern Mediterranean. Copies for use in the military messes were made at Longthorpe (Peterborough) and Inchtuthil (Scotland).

African red slip ware comprised a variety of fine slip-coated forms
and fabrics, manufactured probably at various centres in North
Africa (mostly modern Tunisia) by a samian-derived industry,
and common in the Mediterranean littoral, but reaching Roman
Britain in very small quantities from mid/late I to late IV, and
subsequently imported to the Celtic West during late V and VI.
At Bar Hill on the Antonine Wall potters, perhaps from North
Africa, made vessels in the same tradition in mid II.

Severn Valley wares emerged in the 50s, probably initially in
connection with military supplies to the Gloucester area. They
represent a fusion of traditions, some derived from South-east
Britain, others local native or Roman. Tankards (figure VIII,
168), carinated bowl/beakers, hemispherical bowls and deeper
S-shaped bowls and storage-jars occurred in various fabrics,
usually hard light buff-orange (sometimes grey), with distinctively burnished areas or lines. They emanated from many centres
such as Shepton Mallet (Somerset), near Malvern (Worcester-
shire) and Portway, near Gloucester, the colonial town where
they were first distinguished and formerly called *Glevum ware*.
Severn Valley wares were produced until early/mid IV and
marketed mainly in the Severn Valley and adjacent areas, but
small amounts were supplied intermittently to the western sector
of Hadrian's Wall from *c*.130 to early III and to garrisons in
Scotland in mid II and early III. Immigrant potters, perhaps from
the Gloucester area, also set up near Inveresk (Forth estuary) in
mid II.

The Verulamium region industry (St Albans, Hertfordshire)
consisted of numerous kilns along Watling Street south of the
Roman town, including *Brockley Hill* and *Radlett*. Emerging in
c.48/55, probably with immigrant continental potters, and expanding rapidly, it was soon important, not only for mortaria
(plate 12), but for a variety of flagons, carinated bowls and more
exotic forms, all in a granular white to pink/buff paste (figure IV,
131-5). At peak (70-120) these dominated pottery supplies to
London and adjacent territory and were reaching Midland and
northern military consumers generally in lesser amounts, except
for large quantities of mortaria. By mid II to early/mid III
shrinking production was confined mostly to mortaria for
relatively local purchasers.

The Medway Estuary including **Upchurch.** From the romanisation of native late iron age potting, there developed a major industry in *c.*70, making fine grey, black-coated and burnished tablewares, as well as local kitchen wares. The former included poppy-head and biconical beakers (plate 9), Gallo-Belgic forms, imitation samian (plate 8) and regional varities of flasks and S-shaped bowls. From late I to late II these reached London and the South-east in quantity; from *c.*120 to late II they were shipped to north-eastern frontier garrisons, probably alongside the local black-burnished ware (BB2: see chapter 4). Thereafter, until the industry's collapse in late III, reduced output (mainly globular and indented funnel-mouthed beakers) served local markets only.

3
Mortaria

These general-purpose mixing-bowls, associated with classical modes of food preparation, often had heavy rims for easy gripping and lifting, *trituration grits* on the interior surface to reinforce the vessel and aid pulping, and, normally, pouring-spouts (plate 13). Their production, often linked to that of flagons in I and early II, was sometimes concentrated in the hands of specialist potters.

Early supply of mortaria. Small quantities of *wall-sided* mortaria were first imported from *c.*10 BC for wealthy communities in the South-east. After AD 43, there arrived increasing amounts of wall-sided and flanged mortaria, probably from the Rhineland. The former type (figure VI, 150), usually ungritted but some-times scored internally, was obsolescent by *c.*50/5. Mortarium usage soon spread, no doubt initially through the Roman army. Production in Britain probably began soon after the invasion, but at first imports were significant. Some continental makers impressed their name-stamps or trademarks across the rim near the spout, a tradition adopted in many Romano-British work-shops (plate 12), until the practice gradually ceased during II.

Four major potteries supplied over 50 per cent of the mortaria in Britain in mid to late I: the **Verulamium region industry** from *c.*48/55 (chapter 2); Q. Valerius Secundus, Q. Valerius Veranius and associates following similar traditions in North-east France (usually termed **Groups I and II**); workshops in **Gallia Belgica** (probably near *Bavai* and *Amay*); and the **Atisii at Aoste,** Isère, South France (figure VI, 153). Of the two most successful, Verulamium mortaria (figure IV, 131-2; plate 12) were more concentrated in the London region, and inland in the Midlands and North, while Group I and II products were distributed coastally, with perhaps the bulk in southern and south-western England. The latter were cream or buff with wide, often flattish rims, well made spouts, internal scoring and tiny flint gritting spread over the interior and sometimes on the rim (figure VI, 152). Smaller amounts of unstamped mortaria also arrived in mid I from the *Eifel* region, Germany (figure VI, 151), and from *Central Gaul.*

The Hartshill and Mancetter factories. The first Romano-British workshops began to decline in importance early in II, but by *c.*100 a new industry had been set up at Mancetter/Hartshill, near Nuneaton, Warwickshire, which was to become of premier importance in the production of mortaria. A study of the fabrics and stamps suggests that some potters from Verulamium region workshops, including G. Attius Marinus (previously at Colchester and Radlett), migrated there *c.*100. These vast industrial complexes with their numerous potters soon became one of the main suppliers to the North, particularly to the army, and in addition dominated the central and west Midlands. A distinctive fine hard white 'pipe-clay' fabric and medium-sized red-brown and/or blackish grits, applied on the interior only, were characteristic. Some of the first products resembled the Verulamium region's output (*cf* plate 12; figure IV, 132), but by late II the current fashion was for smaller flanges, less hooked and more flaring, and increasingly prominent bead-rims (figure VII, 157).

Towards the end of II, coinciding with a streamlining and intensification of mortarium production (and a decline in kitchen-ware manufacture), the potters discontinued name-stamping and began to make *hammer-head* rims; these were sometimes decorated with horizontal grooving (*reeding*), or occasionally *painted*, usually with simple geometric patterns (figure VII, 157-8). From early IV competition from Crambeck mortaria (chapter 5, figure XVII, 238-41) gradually eroded Mancetter/Hartshill's long-distance trade in the North until it was reduced to a local scale.

Second-century centres in northern England and North Wales. At first some manufacture was in the hands of the army, or civilians working in military traditions often under its aegis, as in the tileries at **Holt** (Clwyd), **Muncaster** (Cumbria), **Grimscar** (Huddersfield) and **York**. Mortaria from the last are usually orange-brown, sometimes with a cream slip.

Independent potters were also lured northwards by potential military demand. One from **Wroxeter** may have migrated to Stockton Heath, **Wilderspool,** Cheshire, a factory active until *c.*165. In mid II some of the Wilderspool craftsmen probably moved to **South-west Scotland**, working there until early III. These workshops all made so-called *Raetian mortaria*, typified by an orange paste, lug handles, an angular cut-out spout, a glossy red-brown slip, applied only on the top of the flange, rim and internal concave moulding, and trituration grits confined to

below this feature (figure VI, 154). These and mortaria related in
finish but more conventional in *form* were made and used mainly
in the west of Britain.

At **Rossington Bridge**, South Yorkshire, Sarrius, a Mancetter
manufacturer, opened a new workshop in *c.*140-50 (figure VII,
155). It was part of a large industry near Doncaster (including
Cantley), selling moderate quantities of mortaria and other wares
to North-east England and Scotland in mid to late II and
sporadically later, and larger quantities more locally from mid II
to IV. The mortaria, often similar in profile to the Midland
products, were usually red-brown with a thick grey core, a cream
slip and ironstone grits.

Lincoln was also a centre for mortarium production. Vitalis'
workshop traded with North-east England and locally in *c.*90-120.
The Antonine Wall and North-east England were the main
markets for the output of kilns north of Lincoln at **South Carlton**
in *c.*140-70 (figure IX, 174). A slightly sandy cream fabric, with
darker slip and mixed grits, was typical of both factories. In late
III and IV the **Swanpool** kilns (south of Lincoln) made coarse
brownish mortaria with a white slip and black ironstone grits
(figure XIII, 212); they were thinly distributed in Yorkshire and
North Lincolnshire, but abundant locally.

Potteries were even set up on the northern frontiers, as at
Corbridge in mid to late II, and near several forts on the
Antonine Wall in mid II. Only a few continental mortaria now
reached these consumers, but British factories continued to
provide large quantities until late IV/early V.

Second-century centres in southern England and South Wales. A
major industry around **Oxford** emerged, probably following the
migration of potters from the Verulamium area. Between *c.*100
and 170 they impressed mostly illegible trademark stamps on
mortaria in a fine cream fabric, often with a pink or orange tinge
(figure XII, 197). The distinctive multicoloured (predominantly
pink) translucent quartz internal grits were the hallmark of
Oxfordshire mortaria both then and later, when their distribution
spread beyond the South Midlands (chapter 5; figure XII, 198-9,
202).

Serving Wales, the Marches and the Bristol Channel area in
late I and II were several centres. One, at **Caerleon** (Gwent),
perhaps initially associated with the Second Augusta Legion
there, made smooth red-coated mortaria, sometimes illegibly
stamped, and gritted with white quartz.

From mid II to late III another factory, perhaps near **Cirencester**, produced mortaria in a coarse orange-brown fabric with a blue core, a cream slip and grits of flint and pink quartz. These, and flagons and jars from the same source, were traded mainly in North Wiltshire, Gloucestershire, Avon, Somerset and Dorset. An industry with more restricted markets operated somewhere in the **Surrey/East Sussex** area in mid/late II and III.

Colchester had been a thriving production centre since early I. In mid/late I to early II the hard white or cream flint-gritted mortaria, often stamped by such firms as the Sexti Valerii, sold particularly well in East Anglia and the South-east, but thinly to the Midlands and North (figure X, 179). Colchester's boom period was, however, from *c.*140 to early III, when both the flanged and the distinctively grooved wall-sided vessels, sometimes impressed with herringbone trademarks (135-75) or name-stamps (150-190/200), spread beyond the traditional south-eastern marketing area and were shipped in quantity to military consumers in Scotland and North-east England alongside other products (chapter 4; figure X, 186-7). Declining output in III reached East Anglia alone, until production ceased in *c.*270.

From mid II to early III a related industry with stylistically similar products (sometimes bearing herringbone stamps) supplied North Kent on a smaller scale, probably from **Canterbury.** Herringbone-stamped mortaria were also made at **Brampton,** Norfolk, in mid to late II and sold mainly in Norfolk. Only a very small proportion of the many herringbone mortaria in Scotland and North-east England are from these two sources.

Imports. Beginning in mid II, mortaria from the **Rhineland** arrived, mostly in the South and South-west, but were widely distributed in small quantities over the rest of Britain. Typical forms included almost wall-sided vessels with an internally swelling rim in a hard cream-white fabric, sometimes with a pink core, and tiny multicoloured crystalline grits over the whole internal surface (figure VII, 159).

At **Soller,** Kreis Düren, Germany, the potter Verecundus (*c.*170-200+) made huge cream, finely sandy, flanged mortaria with brown trituration grits, perhaps intended for use in bakeries (figure VII, 160). These, together with unstamped lighter-weight (probably slightly later) wall-sided and flanged vessels from the same kiln site, were destined for markets mainly in the Rhineland and Britain, though most of Verecundus' stamps are recorded from the latter. After early/mid III, however, Britain was essentially self-sufficient in mortaria.

The late centres. Following a peak in mid to late II, there was a marked decline in the total number of mortarium producers in Britain. An exceptional area was **East Anglia,** where *Pakenham* (Suffolk) and a number of other small workshops, manufacturing in traditions influenced by Colchester and the Nene Valley, catered for relatively local needs in III and early IV (figure XVIII, 245). Elsewhere, a few large production centres gradually dominated extensive regions. Some, such as the **Crambeck** (North Yorkshire), **Swanpool** and **New Forest** factories (chapter 5), were newly established after mid III. Others, such as **Mancetter/Hartshill,** the **Nene Valley** and **Oxfordshire** (chapter 5), were earlier industries which underwent massive expansion in III and IV.

4
The early second century onwards

By *c*.120 the impact on Romano-British pottery of the early exotic types introduced for the army of conquest had diminished considerably. Although there continued to be links with the continent, cooking-wares in particular became essentially insular. The closure of most military works depots in *c*.120 and subsequent reliance by the garrisons on pottery supplies from civilian sources also contributed to the upsurge of a number of industries. Civilian markets burgeoned too, encouraging the growth of regional centres supplying smaller settlements and villas.

In the long term, perhaps the most significant developments in II were the emergence of the black-burnished ware industries and the establishment of major production centres for colour-coated wares. A stimulus for the latter may have been the temporary shortage of samian in Britain from *c*.90 to *c*.130/40. Even so, the fashion for such tablewares was to outlast samian importation and almost certainly contributed to its general decline in early to mid III. The increasing popularity of colour-coated beakers from Gaul and Germany from late I must also have stimulated British production. Significantly, the pottery styles and kiln structures of the two main Romano-British producers, Colchester and the Nene Valley, suggest the early involvement of craftsmen from the Rhineland, Moselle or North-east France.

Cologne colour-coated wares, first imported from *c*.80, comprised a range of fine beakers with a grooved or delicately moulded (*cornice*) rim, an indented or bag-shaped body and a gently rounded girth (forms superseding the high-shouldered ovoid prototypes from earlier workshops). They had a powdery white fabric, a thick dark grey, often lustrous slip and barbotine scales or rough-cast decoration of crushed clay particles starting a little below the rim; the later technique continued until late II (figure IV, 140).

Sales to Britain increased in II as the products diversified. Globular or waisted rough-cast beakers with a short upward-curving neck and plain rim were introduced. From *c*.120/30 more angular bag-beaker forms appeared, decorated *en barbotine* with a hare or stag chased by hounds (*hunt cups;* plate 16) or with rouletted bands. Against strong competition from similar Romano-British wares, Cologne beakers were ubiquitous, capturing the major share of the British market until early III.

Other imported beakers (mostly late I to early/mid II) are distinguished by different fabrics. Widespread in Britain, and probably from the Argonne, France, were fine orange, more cylindrical rough-cast cornice-rimmed beakers, with a glossy blue-black coat, 'wipe-marks' behind the rim, and sometimes a shoulder groove (figure IV, 139). Less frequent but generally similar was a more globular beaker, possibly from the Middle Rhineland or East Gaul. A softer, fine micaceous pale orange-buff fabric, a pale brown-orange slip and sparser clay rough-casting were typical.

Colchester, successively pre-conquest tribal capital and entrepot for imported pottery, legionary fortress and colonial town, had long been an important manufacturing centre for both specialist and kitchen wares (chapter 3). About 120, among other products, the Colchester kilns began to make cornice-rimmed beakers with crushed clay rough-casting, copying contemporary imports. They were bag-shaped or indented, with an orange-red sandy fabric slipped matt reddish-brown or dark grey (figure IX, 183). A few reached Hadrian's Wall. By mid II the expanding repertoire included flagons, mica-dusted jugs, colour-coated *castor boxes* and a wide variety of beaker-forms decorated with rouletting, applied scales or barbotine motifs such as hunting scenes, public shows (plate 17), phallic symbols, deities and strange, perhaps Celtic, masked men engaged in ritual mysteries. Their distribution, not yet fully studied, apparently encompassed London, East Anglia and southern England, as well as the Antonine Wall and the North-east, whither they were shipped alongside Colchester mortaria (chapter 3; figure X). Despite the loss of northern military markets in early III, Colchester continued to supply diminishing quantities of mortaria and colour-coated vessels to East Anglia and the South-east until late III, when Nene Valley tablewares gained dominance in the region. Production of grey wares for local consumers may have survived a little longer.

The Lower Nene Valley. Pottery had been produced in the area since mid I, when kilns were set up for the military at Longthorpe. In I and II, Middle and Upper Nene Valley workshops made native calcite-gritted vessels and romanised grey wares, mostly regional types, but including Gallo-Belgic derived

platters, *London ware* with impressed stamps, and sandy cream
mortaria. From mid/late II a major industrial complex developed
between Wansford and Peterborough, for several miles along the
north bank of the river Nene (Cambridgeshire), with its centre at
the Roman town of *Durobrivae* (Water Newton). Often called
castor ware after the parish in which it was first recognised, the
main products comprised a great variety of table-forms in a fine
off-white to reddish-yellow fabric with a black to brown-red
colour-coat. They included jugs, flagons, *castor boxes* and
indented, bag-shaped or ovoid beakers, plain or cornice-rimmed,
cordoned, rouletted or with applied scales (figure XI, 189-94).
Best known are those with barbotine hunting scenes, gladiators
or scrolls (mid II to early/mid III), or with elaborate trails of
berries and foliage painted in thick white overslip, popular in III
and also in IV when motifs were steadily simplified (plate 18;
figure XI, 193). Nene Valley wares attained their widest and most
concentrated circulation (covering most of Britain) in III, when
importation of the rival, and almost indistinguishable, Cologne
beakers had ceased, and before Oxfordshire tablewares had
gained dominance in the South. The mortaria, similarly but more
thinly distributed (especially in the South and South-west), were
pale buff in fabric and gritted with black ironstone, and they often
had a reeded flange (plate 19). In III to IV, following current
trends, the Nene Valley potters also made *late imitation samian*
bowls in a white fabric with a red-brown colour-coat, and cream
late parchment wares with red-brown painted motifs (chapter 5;
figure XI, 195). Output had always included pale grey kitchen
wares for more local use (figure XI, 196), but in late III finer
colour-coated versions of these forms went into production. They
were widespread until early V, even holding their own on a
reduced scale against fierce competition in the north from
Crambeck Wares and in the south from Oxfordshire products
(chapter 5).

Other Romano-British colour-coated wares were more short-
lived:

  South Carlton (Lincolnshire) kilns made pink-buff beakers
with a purplish-brown colour-coat and sand rough-casting, as well
as cream mortaria (chapter 3; figure IX, 173). The output
reached the Antonine Wall and north-eastern markets within the
period *c.*140-70.

  Cornice-rim beakers with rough-casting, from workshops at
*Great Casterton,*Leicestershire, and *Wilderspool,* Cheshire, and

with combed or applied decoration, from a centre west of *Wanborough,* Wiltshire (figure V, 147), apparently circulated more locally in II.

'Rhenish' ware. Two common varieties are now distinguished, neither of which was manufactured in the Rhineland:

Moselle Ware (*Moselkeramik*), shipped from Trier, Germany, was widespread in Britain, mainly from late II to mid III. It is identifiable from its thin red-brown cortex with a dark grey core, a lustrous dark grey-black slip and diagnostic profiles. These, frequently copied by Romano-British producers, included funnel-mouthed indented and bulbous beakers, rouletted, or sometimes painted with thick white overslip scrolls and berries. The well known *motto-beakers* (plate 10), of which some arrived after mid III, combined this decoration with ornately lettered words forming phrases such as DA MERUM (Give me pure wine!), BIBE (Drink up!) and other less refined instructions.

Central Gaulish black-coated ware (*black samian*), also widely distributed in Britain from shortly after mid II to mid III, was made at Lezoux (Central France) and probably at other samian factories. Markedly different in forms and fabric, it was characterised by ovoid rouletted beakers and small cups, both with a 'bung-foot' (figure IX, 176-7), and a micaceous red samian-like fabric, a thin black iridescent slip, and sometimes barbotine leaf, dot and corn-ear motifs.

North Gaulish grey wares, noted in small quantities in Britain, mainly on eastern coastal sites, probably originated from the Artois-Picardy region of northern France in II to early III. The beakers with a long funnel-mouth (*vases troconiques;* figure IX, 178), carinated bowls and segmental dishes had a light blue-grey granular fabric and a thin grey slip, over-burnished in bands (*bandes lustrées*) on the neck, rim or interior. Similar grey to pale orange, rouletted, *pentice-moulded beakers* (figure XI, 193) probably emanated from the same area in early III.

Black-burnished ware. Military orders probably caused the sudden rise to prominence of this type of pottery. Two classes of fabric are distinguishable: one, **BB1,** with its origins among the iron age (Durotrigan) peoples of Dorset, is black and gritty and was hand-made and burnished in facets; the other, **BB2,** is greyish, finer and wheel-thrown, with a silky, more regular surface. It was produced from early II, in imitation of BB1, by the romanised native industries of the Thames Estuary (particularly on the Cliffe peninsula of North-west Kent). About 120, the producers of BB1 (around Poole Harbour), whose output had hitherto found its main markets in Dorset and Devon, undertook to supply quantities to the army on Hadrian's Wall and its hinterland; about 140, BB2 was the subject of a similar arrangement for Scotland. Both wares subsequently reached the northern garrisons until *c*.250/60 when the already declining BB2 deliveries ceased. At first more BB1 and (temporarily) small quantities of Thames Estuary lid-seated jars filled the gap (figure IX, 172), but from the 270s until *c*.367 (when supply to the North terminated) BB1 was gradually ousted by the products of the burgeoning East Yorkshire potteries (chapter 5).

The North excepted, BB2 had never been common outside eastern England, but, following its demise in mid/late III, BB1 now achieved its maximum distribution — abundant over most of the province, but sparser in the East. There, many workshops were turning out good-quality grey-ware copies. By late IV, however, BB1's own markets had contracted to an area comprising mainly South Wales and South-west England, beyond which other cooking wares gained dominance (chapter 5).

Secondary BB1 factories existed at Rossington Bridge (Doncaster) and in the North Somerset marshes, the former exporting to the northern frontiers in mid to late II. Others remain unlocated.

The standard range of black-burnished vessel-forms was fairly uniform, with only minor variations from fabric to fabric; they were frequently imitated by potteries over much of Britain. The thin-walled *cooking-pots* were clearly for use over a fire or oven, and the development of their shape and decoration is a useful chronological guide. In II they were squat, with a short neck and upward-flaring rim (figures VIII, 161; IX, 169); burnishing occurred just inside the rim and on the exterior, except for a broad central band of lightly incised *acute-angled lattice* decoration. In III and IV BB1 vessels became more elongated, with a longer neck and a rim projecting outwards, ultimately well beyond the girth of the pot (plate 11; figure VIII, 162). The lattice, increasingly *obtuse-angled* from *c*.220, was gradually confined to a very much narrower band and, from shortly before mid III, began to be terminated above by a horizontally scored line. A late variety of BB1, apparently produced in the North Somerset marshes and traded mostly in the South-west in mid IV to early V (perhaps on the decline or collapse of the Dorset factories), was more bowl-like in proportions, with a less sharply everted rim, not overhanging the girth, and a narrow band of steeply inclined parallel lines (figure VIII, 163).

The BB1 *bowl* in II was a carinated vessel with a flattened lip and a band of acute-angled lattice (figure VIII, 164). This decoration was steadily superseded from *c.*180 by intersecting arc decoration. From shortly before *c.*200 a groove appeared on the more hooked lip, producing an *incipient bead-rim* (figure VIII, 165); the version of late III-IV was proportionately deeper, with a pronounced *bead-rim and flange* and burnished intersecting arcs (plate 11; figure VIII, 167). BB2 bowls were generally similar, but with wavy-line, lattice or parallel-line decoration and a triangular rim in mid II; the rim became more rounded from *c.*170/80 with a simultaneous loss of decoration (figure IX, 170-1). A simple platter, often referred to as a 'dog-dish', perhaps also used as a lid, was popular in both industries (plate 11; figure VIII, 166).

5
The mid third to fourth century

Because of a dearth of closely dated deposits in Britain in the first half of III, there is some doubt which pottery should be assigned to this period. In early to mid III there was a peak in the total number of workshops, perhaps due to increased rural prosperity. After mid III, however, many gradually closed and in IV there were fewer but much larger production centres. This may have contributed to a more rapid breakdown of pottery manufacture in early V (chapter 7). The balance of pottery supplies to the North was radically altered by the emergence of the East Yorkshire potteries. Shipments of samian had ceased by mid III; imports thereafter were few. British producers of tablewares adopted new ranges, *late imitation samian (pseudo-samian)* and *late painted parchment wares*. The former initially copied, in form, finish and decoration, the latest East Gaulish samian imports. Later, styles diversified. Decoration was no longer applied by stamped moulds but was impressed directly on to the pot itself. *Late parchment wares*, mostly bowls in pale mortarium-like fabrics, were slip-painted with simple reddish patterns. Flagons and mortaria generally tended to be smaller; beakers and some cooking-pots became proportionately taller, but after mid IV this trend was sometimes reversed. In the South several hand-made grog-tempered wares became prominent from late III (chapter 6). By the end of IV kitchen wares were very limited in range.

The Nene Valley and four other industries dominated fineware production from mid/late III. Minor products such as *Canterbury streak-burnished ware, Pakenham* (Suffolk) colour-coated wares (figure XVIII, 245-6), and *Messingham* (Lincolnshire) copies of colour-coated forms (figure XV, 227) apparently reached more restricted areas; these require further research.

The Oxfordshire industry. Although there had been kilns in the region since mid I, only the mortaria achieved a wide (South Midland) distribution before mid III (chapter 3; figure XII, 197). From *c.*240 manufacture of tablewares burgeoned, until, from mid IV to early V, Oxfordshire output dominated most fineware assemblages south of the Trent. The colour-coated vessels, including *imitation samian,* had a pink-orange micaceous fabric and a reddish or brownish slip. The earliest, appearing in mid to late III, copied Drag 31, 36, 37 and 38 samian bowls, Drag 45 mortaria and contemporary colour-coated flagons and beakers (figure XII, 200, 202-3). By early IV a divergent range of bowls had emerged. Decorative techniques common by mid IV included impressed rosettes and demi-rosettes, comb-stamping and scrolls painted in white overslip (figure XII, 199, 201, 204-5; plate 23).

The *parchment wares,* current from 240, had a similar but thinner distribution. Most popular was a carinated bowl, in a fine white powdery fabric often pinkish in core, painted with red-brown bands on the rim and carination and with concentric designs inside (plate 20). Mortaria in the same fabric, with prominent rims and hooked, rolled-over or squat angular flanges (forms typical of mid III to early V), were widely marketed over southern England and East Anglia (figure XII, 198).

Harston (south of Cambridge), a minor offshoot of the Oxfordshire kilns, made similar mortaria, parchment and red-coated wares, all in a pink-white fabric. They were sparsely distributed in East Anglia in *c.*325 to 350.

Pevensey ware, characterised by an uneven surface, red-orange paste and darker slip, probably came from a small (unlocated) Oxfordshire-derived workshop. The plain, stamped or white slip-painted bowls and jars, restricted in range, all closely corresponded to Oxfordshire output (figure XII, 206). Distribution was confined to the coast of Sussex and east Hampshire, with a floruit in mid/late IV.

The New Forest potteries, operational from *c.*250/60, shared many forms and decorative techniques with the Oxfordshire factories. Their most traded products were, however, fine colour-coated indented, bulbous or bag-shaped beakers, bottle-like flasks and flagons and small bowls (plate 22; figure XIII, 207, and cover photograph), types less important to the Oxfordshire industry. Concentrated in the area immediately adjacent to the kilns, they were thinly distributed over much of England south of the Thames. Fabrics varied from buff to hard blue-grey, and colour-coats from matt red-brown to lustrous purple, reflecting low or high firing temperatures. The earliest decoration comprised rouletting, and barbotine scales or leaves (pre-280/90), horizontal stabbing or incised wavy lines (pre-340), and elaborate geometric motifs in white paint (sometimes within impressed concentric circles). By mid IV vessel-types were fewer and slip-painting was confined to simple scrolls and horizontal lines. In decline by *c.*370, the industry had probably collapsed before the end of IV.

New Forest *imitation samian*, cream-buff with a brownish-orange slip (plate 23), served very restricted markets. Its production followed a progression similar to that of its Oxfordshire counterpart. The *parchment wares*, markedly different from Oxfordshire's output, were also traded less widely. Most typical was a bowl in a harsh sandy off-white fabric, internally flanged and painted with simple orange-red motifs (plate 21). A finer sand-free paste was normal after *c.*340/50. *Mortaria*, some quite similar to Oxfordshire products, occurred in colour-coated and parchment-type fabrics (figure XIII, 208-9). Recognisable from their grey and white flint trituration grits, they sold mainly in adjacent counties. Grey culinary ranges, often identical in form and indistinguishable in fabric from Alice Holt/Farnham wares (see below), served local consumers.

Hadham ware. There had been pottery manufacture in the Hadham area (near the Roman town of Braughing, Hertfordshire) since late I and early II, when grey bowls were traded over distances of up to 30 miles (50 km). In late III production revived. These late tablewares, often distinguished by a hard red fabric with a dark grey core and a smooth red-orange slipped *and* burnished surface, but sometimes fired grey, were concentrated in East Anglia, London and the Thames Estuary, and sporadically further south, in late III to V, particularly after *c.*350. Typical forms included narrow-mouthed handled jars with a frilled rim, face-neck flagons with flattened handles and a 'coal scuttle' profile, bossed and dimpled ('*Romano-Saxon*') bowls, globular beakers and flasks, sometimes with relief-moulded animals (figure XIV, 214-17), late *imitation samian* and mortaria with profiles and gritting similar to contemporary Oxfordshire products. Common types of cooking-vessels in grey burnished ware and rough sandy rilled jars copying Midland shell-gritted wares (see below) had slightly more restricted markets.

The Swanpool workshops formed part of a larger grey-ware industry operating south-west of Lincoln from III onwards and supplying mainly the town and its environs. At peak in mid/late IV, they made mortaria, sometimes with a reeded flange (chapter 3), and dishes, bowls, jugs and face-neck flagons, often in a light red-brown fabric with a self-coloured slip, and rouletting or simple white painted motifs generally similar to late Nene Valley wares (figure XIII, 212-13). Grey kitchen wares, including distinctive lid-seated jars, dominated production.

East Yorkshire grey wares (figure XVI, 232-5), from centres at *Norton* (Malton), North Yorkshire, and the Holme on Spalding Moor area (including *Throlam* and *Hasholme*), North Humberside, hitherto of local significance, began to reach the northern garrisons soon after mid III, but increasingly from late III onwards when their production also commenced at *Crambeck*, south of Malton, North Yorkshire. By the 360s these sand-tempered culinary vessels and local *Knapton/Huntcliffe calcite-gritted wares* (see below) monopolised northern markets, having ousted southern rivals.

Crambeck, working from *c*.290 to early V, also made table-wares and mortaria in a cream fabric, sometimes with an ochre slip. The latter, studded with abundant, often fine, black ironstone grits, had flanged or hammer-head profiles (pre-360/70; figure XVII, 238). Wall-sided and more elaborate hard-fired forms (often polished and painted with red-brown motifs) generally appeared with the emergence of fine parchment-ware production in the 360s and 370s (figure XVII, 239-43; plate 25). Kitchen wares, in a distinctive, fairly fine, pale grey fabric, with a lead-grey burnished surface, included jars with countersunk handles and flanged bowls, sometimes with an internal incised or burnished wavy line (figure XVII, 236-7).

Imports. Small amounts of the following trickled into Britain, mostly in the East and South-east, especially at ports, often perhaps as personal baggage:

Argonne ware, a similar but late descendant of samian, arriving from North-east France mainly in late III to IV, included plain and decorated bowls. The latter were distinguished by horizontal bands of impressed patterns (often squares infilled with diagonals), executed with a *roller stamp* — a roller on which several repeating panels of design had been cut (figure XV, 228).

French late marbled ware (*céramique à l'éponge*), mostly flanged (Drag 38) or carinated bowls, and occasionally beakers, came from the Aquitaine region (South-west France), mainly in late III and IV (figure XV, 229). It had a fine pale yellow fabric and a glossy yellow-orange surface, over which were sponged or dabbed darker blurred foliated blotches or overall marbling.

German late marbled ware (*marmoriete keramik*), rarer and probably a Middle Rhineland product, comprised jugs and two-handled flanged flagons (figure XIV, 218), in a rougher creamy-buff fabric, with a patchy matt orange-red or brown-black sponge-marbled slip (generally late III and IV in Britain).

Mayen ware from the Eifel, Germany, thinly but more widely distributed in Britain, mainly in late III and IV, included squat jars with a pronounced *lid-seating* (figure XV, 225), and bowls with an internally swelling rim (sometimes imitated in Britain; figure XV, 225). Conspicuous by their very hard, pimply, yellow-brown or purple, often 'glassy' fabric, Mayen wares were fired almost to vitrification point.

Kitchen wares. The following regional industries or local native traditions attained wider significance in III and IV:

Midland shell-gritted wares. These cooking-vessels, which had developed from late iron age traditions in the South and East Midlands, became increasingly popular in IV over a much wider area (east of a line from Lincoln to Bath). Characteristic was a shallowly *rilled* S-shaped jar, with a triangular rim, in a dark grey or orange 'soapy' fabric, unevenly fired (perhaps sometimes in clamps) and heavily tempered with particles of shell which often weathered out, leaving a pitted (*vesicular*) effect (figure XIV, 220-1). Kilns are known at Harrold, Bedfordshire, and Lakenheath, Suffolk.

Alice Holt/Farnham kitchen wares, made from shortly before mid I, were sold in bulk to London, Surrey, North Hampshire and north Sussex in late I (figure XV, 222-3). Declining trade in II and III was followed by a resurgence. From *c*.270 to early V the revitalised repertoire reached London and central southern England in increasing quantities, and sporadically beyond. Grey copies of black-burnished ware (BB1) bowls and dishes, bead-rimmed flagons and square-rimmed storage-jars, often with combed lines, burnished bands and zones of white or black slip (figure XV, 224-6), were particularly common. By *c*.330 rilled jars (copying Midland shell-gritted wares) in grey or hard sandy creamy-buff fabrics had appeared. Manufacture of the latter, at Overwey (Farnham) and probably elsewhere, may ultimately have outlasted grey-ware production, continuing into early V.

Dales ware, coarse shell-gritted hand-made cooking-pots with a distinctive wheel-finished rim (figure XVII, 244), emerged in South Humberside from native prototypes in late II. Widespread in Lincolnshire and Yorkshire by early III, small quantities reached the northern frontier from mid/late III. Contemporary hand-made and wheel-thrown copies in sandy and calcite mineral-tempered fabrics (*Dales types*), made at several sites in Lincolnshire, the Humber basin and probably the York area, reached similar markets. By mid IV both varieties had been ousted by competition from Crambeck and Huntcliff wares (below).

Derbyshire ware (plate 26): pimply jars with a deep dished rim to hold a lid in place (*lid-seated*), or a rolled-over rim. It was traded widely in the North Midlands from *c.*140 to mid IV, and small amounts were sold north of Yorkshire, mainly from late III/early IV. The prototypes of the lid-seated form (*pre-Derbyshire ware*) had been introduced into the production area from territories to the south-east by immigrant British craftsmen, who set up workshops to supply the nearby fort at Little Chester, Derby, in late I and early II.

Knapton ware, crude hand-made cooking pots, heavily charged with calcite mineral-grits, and with a rectangular outbent rim (figure XVI, 230), developed in mid I from the native iron age pottery of East Yorkshire. Distribution concentrated in that area, with little change in vessel profiles until mid/late III, when small quantities began to reach the northern frontier. Thereafter quality improved, rims became more curved and export accelerated.

Huntcliff-type cooking-pots (figure XVI, 231) emerged from this typological sequence in mid IV, to become the dominant kitchen ware in the North from the 360s, rivalled only by Crambeck products. Calcite-gritted and hand-made like its ancestors, but with a wheel-turned hooked rim, internally grooved to seat a lid, the type was probably manufactured at several sources, including Knapton, near Malton, North Yorkshire.

6
Local industries

Although the specialist potteries trading over long distances are best known, they were in a minority. Most Romano-British potteries made and supplied simple kitchen vessels just to relatively local consumers. Such wares, often native-derived and regionally distinctive, rarely travelled far from their source. The study of regional and local pottery is, however, still in its infancy and offers great potential. Some of the better known or more recognisable types are outlined here by region:

South-east, Southern and South-west England

Patch Grove ware: coarse grog-tempered bowls and jars with 'Belgic' antecedents, concentrated in west Kent and east Surrey from shortly before mid I to late II.

Canterbury wares (mid/late I to late II): very sandy buff flagons, jugs, carinated bowls, ovoid jars (figure IX, 175) and mortaria, made in the town suburbs by an industry with exotic origins, and marketed mainly in east Kent.

Rowlands Castle ware (Hampshire/Sussex border): these grey everted-rimmed jars with batch-marks incised below the rim (figure V, 146), flagons, flasks and biconical bowls, often with a thin orange slip, were concentrated between the rivers Meon and Lavant from late I to III.

Also serving Sussex were *Wiggonholt/Pulborough* (Arun Valley) kitchen wares and tablewares, including imitation samian (first half of II); and *'Sussex cooking-jar fabrics'*, dark grey and hand-made, with coarse mixed tempering.

Silchester ware from North Hampshire, black/brown burnished bead-rimmed jars and bowls, densely tempered with coarse flint, was common in the vicinity of the town from immediately before the conquest until late I.

Savernake ware, from near Mildenhall, North-east Wiltshire. These pale grey flint- and grog-gritted vessels, mostly jars, were traded over Wiltshire, South Gloucestershire, West Berkshire and North-west Hampshire. Initially partly geared to supply local garrisons in mid I (figure V, 141-2), potting declined in early II. A dispersed offshoot, west of Wanborough, with a more diverse output, including rough-cast colour-coated beakers in II (figure V, 147), flourished until IV.

Congresbury ware, from Avon: flasks, flagons (figure XVIII,

251) and copies of BB1 cooking-pots and dishes, in a light grey fabric with a smoothed surface, were sold mainly in Avon and North-east Somerset in mid/late III to late IV.

Wessex late grog-tempered ware, from South Hampshire: hand-made facet-burnished vessels, perhaps from two unlocated sources mainly copying late black-burnished ware forms (figure XIII, 210), in a fairly hard dark brown/black fabric, heavily tempered with coarse crushed pottery (grog). It was an important component of pottery supply to Hampshire and South Wiltshire and its floruit spanned late III to early V.

Kent late grog-tempered ware (figure XIII, 211), generally similar in character to its Wessex counterpart, but softer and grey/brown, perhaps derived from an earlier local ceramic tradition. Emerging in east Kent in late III and spreading west of the river Medway in IV, it probably constituted the only pottery in use in East Kent at the end of IV and into V.

The Midlands

Apart from *Severn Valley,* early *Oxfordshire* and *Hartshill/ Mancetter* orange and grey kitchen wares, few local products have been studied in detail. Shell-tempered vessels were ubiquitous, from Bedfordshire (*Clapham shelly ware*) to Nottinghamshire (*Trent Valley wares*) and South Lincolnshire (*Bourne ware*). Kilns making sandy romanised grey wares existed at *Elstow*, Bedfordshire (late I-II), in the *South Colne Valley,* Buckinghamshire (including *Fulmer/Hedgerley*) in mid-late I to late II, and at *Wappenbury*, East Warwickshire, from II, but mainly in III and IV. Some potteries, such as *Ecton*, Northamptonshire, tapped sandy and shelly clay sources for different vessel-types.

Eastern England

Rettendon-type wares (Essex): grey flint-tempered regional forms, including bowls (copying BB1) and cavetto-necked jars (figure XVIII, 250), from kilns at Chelmsford and the area to the north-east and south-east, were locally abundant from *c.*280/300 to mid IV, but the industry declined in mid/late IV.

Horningsea ware: grey storage-jars, often with a bi-lobed rim and combed or stabbed decoration, emanated from kilns north-east of Cambridge in II and III.

Wattisfield ware (North Suffolk): an extensive industry working from late I to late IV, with a wide output, typified by a grey fabric high in silver mica (figure V, 143).

Nar Valley ware: *Icenian rusticated jars,* burnished S-shaped bowls with a girth-groove and grooved dishes ultimately copying black-burnished wares, in a hard, granular, dark grey fabric, made at Shouldham, North-west Norfolk (figure XVIII, 248-9) and nearby sites from late II-IV.

'Parisian' stamped wares (plate 15): cordoned beakers, bowls and flasks, in black silky or grey burnished fabrics, decorated with simple impressed stamps such as fern leaves or geometric motifs. Manufactured alongside other wares at Rossington Bridge, Doncaster (South Yorkshire), Market Rasen (Lincoln-shire) and other unlocated sites in Lincolnshire and South Humberside, and distributed in those areas and the Humber basin within the period late I to early III, it was formerly (incorrectly) supposed to originate from the territory of the Parisi (North Humberside).

7
The end of the pottery industries

Details are obscure but it appears that during IV large-scale commercial activity, the function of towns as markets and trade between the four provinces into which Britain was split were already undergoing an overall decline. Between 390 and 402 the removal from Britain of most of the fighting force meant that no new coinage arrived to pay the army. Within about thirty years the use of coins effectively ceased; inevitably local barter replaced long-distance trade. Because the army and its administrators were no longer at hand to uphold political systems and maintain law and order and safe communications, Britain probably split into small self-governing communities.

In pottery production, the general trend towards fewer larger industries in IV probably contributed to a more rapid breakdown in the availability of pottery in V. The major potteries, particularly dependent on settled conditions and a monetary system to sell their wares, must have soon collapsed when such were lacking. Some, such as Mancetter/Hartshill, the New Forest and the Dorset BB1 workshops, were already in decline by the 370s. For the last, not only were northern military sales lost by the 360s, but long-distance civilian markets had contracted too. Some Nene Valley wares still reached the frontier after c.367; perhaps the new Yorkshire coastal installations ensured safe transit for these and northbound East Yorkshire wares. The Oxfordshire potteries, apparently still flourishing in early V, had collapsed well before the local Saxon settlement of mid V. Some smaller, less sophisticated industries (perhaps increasing in some areas, as with Kent grog-tempered ware), still mainly dependent on local markets, would have been in a better position to survive longer than the major factories. Unfortunately, the scarcity of coinage and other artefacts datable to within V makes a complex situation difficult to interpret.

In the eastern half of England hand-made pottery of continental and local origin appears with the Saxon settlers who were arriving in this region from late IV onwards. In the South and West coarse hand-made vessels, often imitating late Roman forms, and made of clay incorporating chopped vegetation (*grass-tempered ware:* plate 27), appear to have been made from V onwards, but only in small quantities; elsewhere people must have used wood or leather substitutes.

8
Kilns

Before the Roman invasion most pottery was fired in surface bonfires or pit-clamps. Some potteries, such as the BB1 workshops, continued to use this technology throughout the Roman period. Permanent kiln structures were introduced at the Roman conquest. They generally comprised a stokehole and flue in which the fire was situated, and an adjacent sunken furnace-chamber, lined with clay, whence the hot air passed upwards through a vented clay floor to an oven in which the pots were stacked (plate 28). Such a furnace chamber often incorporated, as a permanent part of its structure, supports for the oven floor and its load of pots — for example one or more pedestals, a tongue protruding from the back of the chamber, pilasters, corbels or piers, or an internal ledge moulded into the kiln wall. Kiln structures can reflect the origins of potters as much as their products. For example, large rectangular kilns with a massive tongue or pier supports and a long flue were introduced from the continent by potters working for the conquest-period army.

More ephemeral kilns — surface-built or shallowly set temporary structures, probably turf-walled, with reusable prefabricated furniture — have been recognised in the East Midlands, East and South-east England. Such furniture often comprised fired clay pedestals of dumb-bell or slab-like shape and cigar-shaped bars. Probably continental late iron age in origin, this simple technology may have reached eastern England at about the time of the Roman invasion or up to a century before, perhaps concomitant with the introduction of the potter's wheel. The circumstances are unclear, but some immigrant potters following in the wake of the conquest-period army were still building kilns in this basic tradition.

Permanent kilns without a raised oven floor and with a single flue or two opposing flues are also known, particularly in the non-specialist potteries such as Wattisfield and Alice Holt. These may represent the romanisation of native clamp-firing techniques.

Kiln sites yield distinctive assemblages. Clay rings and other items aided the stacking of the pots being fired. The top of the oven was probably insulated by turves over-plastered with clay, at least in the later stages of a firing (see captions to the cover photograph and figure 28); flat grass-marked clay fragments survive from this process. T-shaped ovens of the type often associated with corn-drying or malting were used to dry pots before firing. Other features from kiln complexes include potters' workshops, compartments for storing clay, wells, claypits and puddling holes. Much more large-scale excavation is needed to locate such features.

9
Further reading

Anderson, A. C., and Anderson, A. S. (editors). *Roman Pottery Research in Britain and North-west Europe. Papers Presented to Graham Webster.* British Archaeological Reports International Series 123, 1981.

Arthur, P., and Marsh, G. *Early Fine Wares in Roman Britain.* British Archaeological Reports British Series 57, 1978.

De la Bédoyère, Guy. *Samian Ware.* Shire Publications, 1988.

Detsicas, A. (editor). *Current Research in Romano-British Coarse Pottery.* Council for British Archaeology Research Report 10, 1973.

Dore, K., and Greene, K. (editors). *Roman Pottery Studies in Britain and Beyond. Papers Presented to John Gillam, July 1977.* British Archaeological Reports Supplementary series, 30, 1977.

Fulford, M. G. *New Forest Roman Pottery.* British Archaeological Reports 17, 1975.

Gillam, J. P. *Types of Roman Coarse Pottery Vessels in Northern Britain.* Oriel Press, third edition 1971. The author subsequently modified his views about the dating of pottery of later II and III, generally placing material with dates assigned to this period up to twenty years earlier.

Gillam, J. P. 'Coarse Fumed Ware in North Britain and Beyond'. *Glasgow Archaeological Journal* 4 (1976), 57-90. Updated chronology for BB1.

Greene, K. T. *Report on the Excavations at Usk 1965-76. The Pre-Flavian Fine Wares.* University of Wales Press, 1979.

Howe, M. D., Perrin, J. R., and Mackreth, D. F. *Roman Pottery from the Nene Valley: a guide.* Peterborough City Museum Occasional Paper 2, 1980.

Lyne, M. A. B., and Jefferies, R. S. *The Alice Holt/Farnham Roman Pottery Industry.* Council for British Archaeology Research Report 30, 1979.

Peacock, D. P. S. *Pottery in the Roman World: an Ethnoarchaeological Approach.* Longman, 1982.

Peacock, D. P. S., and Williams, D. F. *Amphorae and the Roman Economy: an Introductory Guide.* Longman, 1986.

Sheppard, A. O. *Ceramics for the Archaeologist.* Carnegie Institution of Washington, 1956; reprinted 1974.

Swan, V. G. *The Pottery Kilns of Roman Britain.* Royal Commission on Historical Monuments Supplementary Series 5, 1984.

Webster, G. (editor). *Romano-British Coarse Pottery: a Student's Guide.* Council for British Archaeology Research Report 6, third edition 1976. Extensive references, but some parts now rather dated.

Webster, P. V. *Roman Samian Ware. Background Notes.* Department of Extra-Mural Studies, University College, Cardiff, 1983. Excellent value.

Young, C. J. *The Roman Pottery Industry of the Oxford Region.* British Archaeological Reports 43, 1977.

Young, C. J. (editor). *Guidelines for the Processing and Publication of Roman Pottery from Excavations.* Directorate of Ancient Monuments and Historic Buildings Occasional Paper 4. Department of the Environment, London, 1980.

A regional selection of excavation reports and papers containing substantial quantities of pottery (excluding those dependent on microfiche):

Bidwell, P. T. *the Legionary Bath-house and Forum at Exeter*. Exeter Archaeological Reports I. Exeter City Council and University of Exeter, 1979.

Bidwell, P. T. *The Roman Fort of Vindolanda*. Historic Buildings and Monuments Commission for England Archaeological Report 1, 1985.

Brown, A. E., Woodfield, C., *et al.* 'Excavations at Towcester, Northants: the Alchester Road Suburb'. *Northamptonshire Archaeology* 18 (1983), 43-140.

Bushe-Fox, J. P. *Reports on the Excavation of the Roman Fort at Richborough, Kent. I-IV*. Reports of the Research Committee of the Society of Antiquaries of London VI, VII, X and XVI; 1926, 1928, 1932 and 1949.

Bushe-Fox, J. P. *Excavations on the Site of the Roman Town at Wroxeter, Shropshire, I-III*. Reports of the Research Committee of the Society of Antiquaries of London I, II and IV; 1913, 1914 and 1916.

Down, A., and Rule, M. *Chichester Excavations I;* Down, A. *Chichester Excavations II, III, IV, V*. Chichester Excavations Committee. Phillimore, 1971, 1974, 1979 and 1981.

Elsdon, S. M. *Parisian Ware*. VORDA Research Series 4. VORDA, High-worth, Wiltshire, 1982.

Frere, S. S. *Verulamium Excavations I-III*. Reports of the Research Committee of the Society of Antiquaries of London XXVIII, XLI, 1972 and 1983; Oxford University Committee for Archaeology Monograph I, 1984.

Going, C. J. *The Mansio and Other Sites in the South-eastern Sector of Caesaromagus: the Roman Pottery*. Chelmsford Archaeological Trust Report 3.2: Council for British Archaeology Research Report 62, 1987.

Hawkes, C. F. C., and Hull, M. R. *Camulodunum*. Report of the Research Committee of the Society of Antiquaries of London XIV, 1947.

Hinchliffe, J., and Green, C. S. *Excavations at Brancaster 1975 and 1977*. East Anglian Archaeology 23. Norfolk Archaeological Unit, 1985.

Jarrett, M. G., and Wrathmell, S. *Whitton, an Iron Age and Roman Farmstead in South Glamorgan*. University of Wales Press, 1981.

Johnson, S. *Burgh Castle, Excavations by Charles Green, 1958-61*. East Anglian Archaeology 20. Norfolk Archaeological Unit, 1983.

Miller, L., Schofield, J., Rhodes, M., *et al. The Roman Quay at St Magnus House, London. Excavation at New Fresh Wharf, Lower Thames Street, London, 1974-78*. London and Middlesex Archaeological Society. Special Paper 8, 1986.

Partridge, C. *Skeleton Green*. Britannia Monograph Series 2, 1981.

Potter, T. W. *Romans in North-west England*. Cumberland and Westmorland Antiquarian and Archaeological Society Research Series I, 1979.

Rahtz, P. A., and Greenfield, E. *Excavations at Chew Valley Lake, Somerset*. Department of the Environment Archaeological Reports 8. HMSO, 1977.

Stead, I. M. *Excavations at Winterton Roman Villa and other Roman Sites in North Lincolnshire, 1958-67*. Department of the Environment Archaeological Reports 5. HMSO, 1968.

Stead, I. M., and Rigby, V. *Baldock*. Britannia Monograph Series 7, 1986.

Wacher, J. S., and McWhirr, A. D. *Early Roman Occupation at Cirencester*. Cirencester Excavations I. Cirencester Excavation Committee, 1982.

Webster, P. V. 'Severn Valley Ware: A Preliminary Study'. *Transactions of the Bristol and Gloucestershire Archaeological Society* 94 (1976), 18-46.

10
Museums

Those listed have extensive Roman collections but are only a regional selection; in addition many smaller local museums both in towns and on Roman sites contain relevant displays. Perhaps the best way to learn about and handle pottery is to volunteer to wash and mark it for an excavation or museum, since the difference in appearance between surface finds of weathered sherds and freshly excavated unabraded pottery can be remarkable. Intending visitors are advised to find out the times of opening before making a special journey.

Ashmolean Museum of Art and Archaeology, Beaumont Street, Oxford OX1 2PH. Telephone: Oxford (0865) 278000.

British Museum, Great Russell Street, London WC1B 3DG. Telephone: 01-636 1555.

Cambridge University Museum of Archaeology and Anthropology, Downing Street, Cambridge CB2 3DZ. Telephone: Cambridge (0223) 337733.

Carlisle Museum and Art Gallery, Tullie House, Castle Street, Carlisle, Cumbria CA3 8TP. Telephone: Carlisle (0228) 34781.

Castle Museum, Norwich, Norfolk NR1 3JU. Telephone: Norwich (0603) 611277 extension 279.

Chichester District Museum, 29 Little London, Chichester, West Sussex PO19 1PB. Telephone: Chichester (0243) 874683.

Colchester and Essex Museum, The Castle, Colchester, Essex CO1 1TJ. Telephone: Colchester (0206) 712490.

Corbridge Roman Site Museum, Corbridge, Northumberland. Telephone: Corbridge (043 471) 2349.

Corinium Museum, Park Street, Cirencester, Gloucestershire GL7 2BX. Telephone: Cirencester (0285) 5611.

Devizes Museum, 41 Long Street, Devizes, Wiltshire SN10 1NS. Telephone: Devizes (0380) 77369.

Doncaster Museum and Art Gallery, Chequer Road, Doncaster, South Yorkshire DN1 2AE. Telephone: Doncaster (0302) 734287.

Dorset County Museum, High Street West, Dorchester, Dorset DT1 1XA. Telephone: Dorchester (0305) 62735.

Gloucester City Museum and Art Gallery, Brunswick Road, Gloucester GL1 1HP. Telephone: Gloucester (0452) 24131.

Grosvenor Museum, 27 Grosvenor Street, Chester, Cheshire CH1 2DD. Telephone: Chester (0244) 21616, 313858 or 316944.

Ipswich Museum, High Street, Ipswich, Suffolk IP1 3QH. Telephone: Ipswich (0473) 213761 or 213762.

Jewry Wall Museum of Archaeology, St Nicholas Circle, Leicester. Telephone: Leicester (0533) 544766 or 554100 extension 3023.

Lincoln City and County Museum, Broadgate, Lincoln LN2 1HQ. Telephone: Lincoln (0522) 30401.

Museum of London, London Wall, London EC2Y 5HN. Telephone: 01-600 3699.

National Museum of Scotland, Queen Street, Edinburgh EH2 1JD. Telephone: 031-225 7534.

National Museum of Wales, Cathays Park, Cardiff, South Glamorgan CF1 3NP. Telephone: Cardiff (0222) 397951.

Peterborough City Museum and Art Gallery, Priestgate, Peterborough, Cambridgeshire PE1 1LF. Telephone: Peterborough (0733) 43329.

Reading Museum and Art Gallery, Blagrave Street, Reading, Berkshire RG1 1QH. Telephone: Reading (0734) 55911 extension 2242.

Rowley's House Museum, Barker Street, Shrewsbury, Shropshire SY1 1QT. Telephone: Shrewsbury (0743) 61196.

Royal Museum and Art Gallery, High Street, Canterbury, Kent CT1 2JE. Telephone: Canterbury (0227) 452747.

Somerset County Museum, Taunton Castle, Castle Green, Taunton, Somerset TA1 4AA. Telephone: Taunton (0823) 55504.

Verulamium Museum, St Michaels, St Albans, Hertfordshire AL3 4SW. Telephone: St Albans (0727) 54659, 59919 or 66100 extension 296.

Winchester City Museum, The Square, Winchester, Hampshire. Telephone: Winchester (0962) 68166 extension 269.

Yorkshire Museum, Museum Gardens, York YO1 2DR. Telephone: York (0904) 29745.

Plate 1. Pre-Flavian fine colour-coated imports. (*Left*) Brown-coated cup with rusticated exterior; height 4.5 cm. (*Right*) Brown-coated cup with applied barbotine imbricated scales; height 6 cm. (Both of Lyon origin, *c.*40-75/80.) (*Centre*) Small beaker with glossy honey-coloured slip and barbotine dot decoration from Baetica, Southern Spain, *c.* 40-80; height 7 cm. (Copyright: British Museum.)

Plate 2. Imported red-buff mica-dusted beaker with pushed-out bosses, probably made by a Gallia-Belgica industry in East Gaul or the Rhineland, mid to late I; the high-shouldered globular profile and tiny rim are typical of beakers in mid/late I; height 14.7 cm. (Copyright: British Museum.)

Plate 3. Central Gaulish yellow-green lead-glazed flagon (St Rémy ware) with relief-moulded decoration, *c.*20-75/80; height 14 cm. (Copyright: British Museum.)

Plate 4. (Below) Bowl imitating samian form Drag 37, with dark brown fabric and olive-green lead glaze over thick white painted decoration, produced in South-east Britain, possibly at Staines, *c.*80-120; height 16.5 cm. (Copyright: British Museum.)

Plate 5. Samian bowl form 37 with relief-moulded decoration incorporating the retrograde name stamp (centre) of the important manufacturer CINNAMVS of Lezoux, Central Gaul, *c.*140-75; above the figured decoration is a continuous ovolo and tongue border, a feature of most Drag 37 samian bowls; diameter 25.8 cm. (Copyright: British Museum.)

Plate 6. Fragment of the porous clay mould of the Lezoux potter Drusus 1 (X-3), used in the manufacture of a Drag 37 samian bowl; the rim and base of the bowl would have been added on the potter's wheel after it had been removed from the mould in a semi-hard state, *c.*90-110; diameter 21.5 cm. (RCHME: Crown Copyright.)

Pottery in Roman Britain

Plate 7. Samian ware. (*Left*) Drag 36 dish with *en barbotine* leaves on the rim, diameter 13.2 cm. (*Right*) Drag 33 plain straight-sided cup, diameter 10.1 cm. Both Central Gaulish, second century. (Copyright: British Museum.)

Plate 8. Upchurch ware bowl imitating approximately samian form Drag 30, with compass-scribed semicircles in place of ovolo decoration and groups of combed lines, end of I to early II; height 12.7 cm. (Copyright: British Museum.)

Plate 9. Poppy-head beaker with vertical and lozenge-shaped panels of barbotine-like dots, probably effected by dipping a comb into a thick semi-liquid clay solution; the near-vertical neck and globular body suggest a date from the end of late I to early II; probably made on the Upchurch Marshes; height 17.7 cm. (Copyright: British Museum.)

Plate 10. Moselle 'rhenish ware' motto-beaker with VIVATIS (Long life!) painted on the dark colour-coat in thick white over-slip, and bands of rouletting; the globular funnel-mouthed form is typical of 'rhenish ware' beakers from this source; late II to mid III; height 11.5 cm. (RCHME: Crown Copyright.)

Plate 11. Black-burnished ware Category 1 (BB1). (*Top*) Cooking-pots with sharply everted rim and acute-angled lattice, mid III to IV; heights (left to right) 18 cm, 22 cm, 28 cm. (*Bottom left and right*) Bowls with pronounced bead-rim and flange, late III/IV; diameters 18 cm and 15 cm. (*Bottom centre*) Plain rimmed dish, late II to III; diameter 20 cm. (*Current Archaeology.*)

Plate 12. Verulamium region mortarium with the (incomplete) retrograde stamps CANDIDVS and FECIT impressed on either side of the elaborate protruding spout; the potter Candidus worked at Brockley Hill, Greater London, in c.95-135; the broad outward-hooked flange with an internal beading is typical of the period; height 7.7 cm. (Copyright: British Museum.)

Plate 13. Cast of scene from the Igel Monument, Moselle, Germany, depicting a basement kitchen; in the centre a servant pounds food in a mortarium (with the spout to his right) which is set in a special frame; to the left, vessels are being washed in a trough and metal platters are stacked on edge; on the right, servants are cooking food over a stove; mid III. (Copyright: Rheinisches Landesmuseum, Trier.)

Plate 14. Rusticated ware cooking-pot in grey fabric; mid/late I to early II; height 13.5 cm. (Copyright: British Museum.)

Plate 15. (Left) Parisian ware stamped jar, an exceptionally elaborate form, but the groups of multiple cordons (presumably Gallo-Belgic in ancestry, like the highly burnished fabric) are characteristic of 'parisian ware' vessels; mid/late II to early III; height 18.5 cm. (RCHME: Crown copyright.)

Plate 16. (Below left) Hunt cup, with the relief of a dog chasing a hare applied *en barbotine;* the style and rather squat, yet slightly angular profile of this cornice-rimmed beaker suggest a probable Cologne source; mid II; height 10.7 cm. (Copyright: British Museum.)

Plate 17. (Below right) Colour-coated bag-shaped beaker with a cornice rim, of Colchester manufacture, with the lively scene of a four-horse chariot race depicted *en barbotine*: the potter may well have never seen such a spectacle, since he has depicted the charioteer clad in gladiatorial armour; mid/late II (lower part of vessel restored); height 14.7 cm. (Copyright: British Museum.)

Plate 18. Nene Valley colour-coated wares. (*Left*) Globular jar with scrolls and berries painted in thick white overslip, imitating the decorative style of Moselle 'rhenish ware', III; height 12.3 cm. (*Centre*) Indented beaker with applied scales, early to mid III; height 15.3 cm. (*Right*) Bag-beaker with plain rim and barbotine foliage-scroll decoration, first third of III; height 11.5 cm. (Copyright: British Museum.)

Plate 19. Nene Valley mortarium from a kiln at Stibbington, Cambridgeshire; the black ironstone or iron-slag trituration grits and the straight reeded flange are typical of Nene Valley mortaria from *c*.250 to 350; diameter 27 cm. (Copyright: British Museum.)

Plate 20. Oxfordshire 'parchment ware' bowls with red-brown painted decoration; both types *c*.240-400+, from the kiln site at the Churchill Hospital, Headington, Oxford. (*Left and right*) Diameters 25.5 cm. (*Centre*) Diameter 8.5 cm. (David Carpenter: Oxford Archaelogical Excavation Committee.)

Plate 21. New Forest 'parchment ware' bowl with characteristic internally ledged rim and orange-red decoration painted on the interior; the more gritty texture of the fabric is immediately apparent (compare the corresponding Oxfordshire ware above); *c*.270-340/50; diameter 26 cm. (K. Grinstead.)

Plate 22. New Forest colour-coated wares. (*Left to right*) Jug with finger-depressed spout and sagging, almost angular profile typical of mid to late IV, height 14.7 cm. Globular funnel-mouthed beaker with incised decoration, *c.*260/70-330; height 14.4 cm. Flanged-neck bottle-like flask with white painted panels, *c.*270-350; height 19 cm. Plain-rimmed bag-beaker with stabbed decoration, *c.*260/70-330; height 8.7 cm. Indented beaker with white painted fronds, *c.*300-30/40; height; 15.5 cm. (K. Grinstead.)

Plate 23. Fragments of colour-coated bowls in 'late imitation samian' tradition showing the method of impressing rosettes and demi-rosettes directly on to the vessel. (*Left*) New Forest ware, cream fabric and browny-orange slip, *c.*345-80; rosette diameter 1.4 cm. (*Right*) Oxfordshire ware, pink-orange fabric, red slip, *c.*340-400+; demi-rosette diameter 1.5 cm. (K. Grinstead.)

Plate 24. (Left) Amphora of 'Rhodian type' (Camulodunum Form 184), characterised by a rounded rim, cylindrical neck, peaked rod-like handles and narrow body tapering to a solid spike; the type was in production from the late first century BC to the early second century AD, but this example dates from the mid first century AD when Rhodian wine was supplied to Britain on a large scale, particularly for the army. Height about 97 cm; capacity about 13.5 litres (3 gallons).

Plate 25. (Right) Face-neck flagon in parchment ware with red painted stripes on the body; the female mask would have been made initially in a mould and then luted with clay to the rest of the vessel; Crambeck ware, c.360/70-400+; height 25.5 cm. (RCHME: Crown copyright.)

Plate 26. (Right) Derbyshire ware cooking-pot. Note the pimply fabric texture, especially on the dished interior of the rim, late II to IV; height 25.5 cm. (Derby Museum.)

Plate 27. (Below) Fragment of grass-tempered ware showing typical surface concavities where vegetable matter and seeds incorporated in the fabric have burnt out during firing; probably V or VI+; about 3 cm across. (K. Grinstead.)

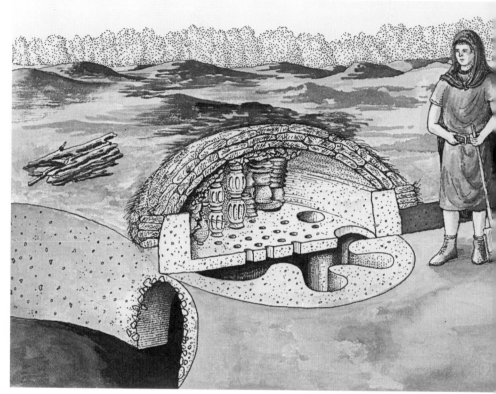

Plate 28. Reconstruction of a pottery kiln of New Forest type with part of the load removed and a section cut away to show the structure. The below-ground furnace chamber is clay-lined, with integral pilasters protruding to support a permanent clay vent-holed oven floor; to the left is the stokehole, with the flue, reinforced with clay and stone. The firing may have commenced with the oven arranged rather like an open-topped cylinder, with turves stacked on a low clay lining-wall; when the pottery load became hard enough to bear the weight, it was probably capped with turves and sherds to aid heat retention. At a late stage in the firing the whole would have been carefully clamped down and sealed with a clay overplastering to produce a reducing (oxygen-free) atmosphere, if grey, black or dark-brown wares were desired. For the same reason the flue was probably simultaneously filled with a fresh supply of wood and then totally blocked up with clay, sand and waste pottery; this ensured that any surviving oxygen in the kiln was completely burnt up.

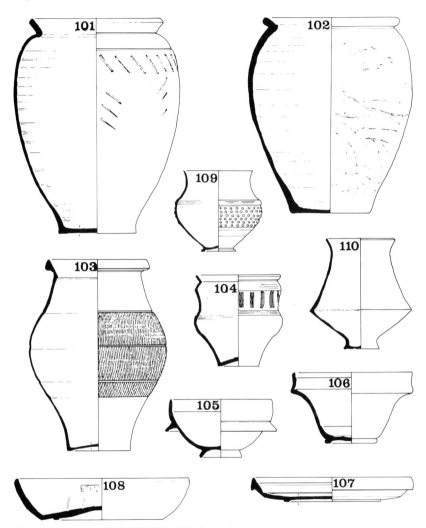

Figure I. GALLO-BELGIC WARES. Scale ¼.
101-2. Central Gaulish pre-conquest imports, mica-dusted on rim and shoulder. 101. Cream jar with barbotine ridges; *c.*10-50 (after Partridge). 102. Red-brown lid-seated jar; *c.*20 BC to AD 10 (after Partridge).
103. Fine white/biscuit-coloured butt-beaker (Camulodunum Form 113), perhaps from North-west France; *c.*10 BC to AD 60 (after Niblett).
104. Girth-beaker made at Chichester by immigrant potters; mid I (after Down).
105-6. Terra nigra cups. 105. Camulodunum Form 58; *c.*35-70. 106. Camulodunum Form 56C; *c.*20-60 (after Rigby). 107. Terra nigra platter (Camulodunum Form 8); *c.*20-60 (after Niblett).
108. Latest terra nigra dish form in Britain (Camulodunum 16); *c.*40-85 (after Greene).
109-10. Egg-shell terra nigra biconical beakers; mid/late I (after Down).

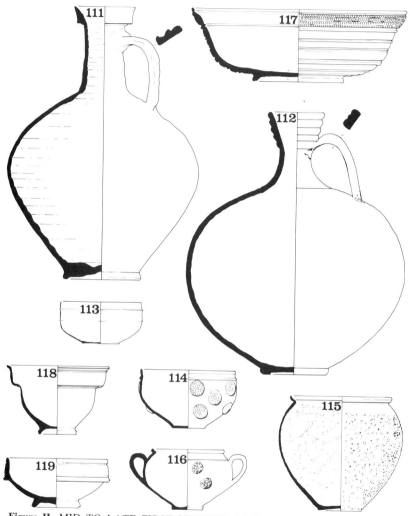

Figure II. MID TO LATE FIRST-CENTURY POTTERY. Scale ¼.
111. Hofheim-type collared flagon, Kingsholm fort, Gloucester (after Darling).
112. Ring-neck flagon from kiln at Otford, Kent. The even, near-vertical neck-rings and angular handle are characteristic of mid I (after Pearce).
113. Italian egg-shell ware cup; *c.*43 to 70 in Britain (after Greene).
114-16. Pre-Flavian fine colour-coated wares, c.43-75. 114. Lyon cup (after Rigby).
115. Lyon rough-cast beaker; the high shoulder and small sharply everted rim are typical of mid/late I (after Darling). 116. Eccles ware cup copying continental form (after Detsicas).
117-19. Imitations of samian forms made by military suppliers in mid/late I. 117. Drag 29 bowl from Kingsholm, Gloucester. 118. Drag 27 cup from Wroxeter, Shropshire (both after Darling). 119. Drag 24/25 cup from Usk, Gwent (after Greene).

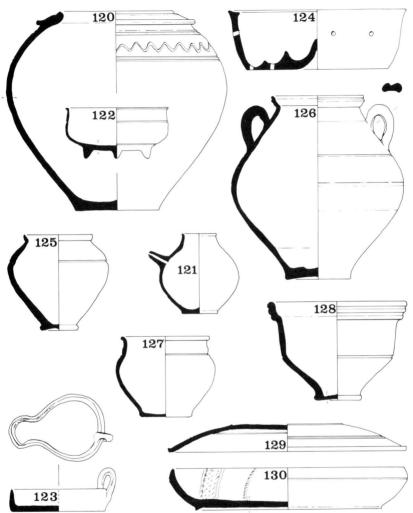

Figure III. POTTERY TYPES INTRODUCED BY THE ARMY OF CONQUEST. Scale ¼.

120, 121. Collared storage-jar and infant feeding-cup or lamp-filler; locally made for Usk fortress by immigrant continental potters; *c.*55-75 (after Greene).

122, 123. Tripod cup and lamp-holder or open lamp; locally made for Wroxeter fortress by continental immigrants; *c.*53/56-60 or 65-71 (after Darling).

124, 125. Cheese-wring and globular beaker; from kilns at Caistor St Edmund, Norfolk; *c.*60/65-80/85

126. 'Honey-jar', supplied to Cirencester garrison; *c.*60-75 (after Rigby).

127, 128. S-shaped bowl; campanulate bowl; both from kilns at Morley, Norfolk, *c.*60/65-75/80.

129,130. Pompeian red ware lid and dish from the Auvergne, Central France, mid to late I (after Greene and Darling).

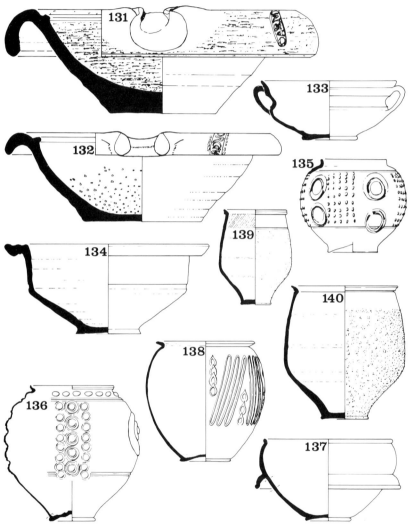

Figure IV. MID FIRST- TO MID SECOND-CENTURY POTTERY. Scale ¼.
131-4. Verulamium region products. 131. Mortarium of Oastrius with typical early profile; *c.*55-80 (after Saunders/Havercroft). 132. Radlett mortarium of Driccius (*c.*100/5-45); form is typical of 120-50 (after Castle). 133. Brockley Hill cup, a continental form; *c.*48/55-70 (after Richardson). 134. Carinated bowl with reeded rim; end of I to mid II (after Tyers).
135. 'Ring and dot' beaker, possibly a Verulamium region product; *c.*50-90 (after Greene).
136-7. Mica-coated wares. 136. Imported beaker with ring-stamped bosses (after Darling). 137. Bowl, probably British; *c.*75-130 (after Frere/Wilson).
138-40. Colour-coated imports. 138. Central Gaulish beaker; late I to early II (after Greene). 139. Rough-cast cornice-rimmed beaker possibly from the Argonne. 140. Cologne ware cornice-rimmed beaker (both after Anderson).

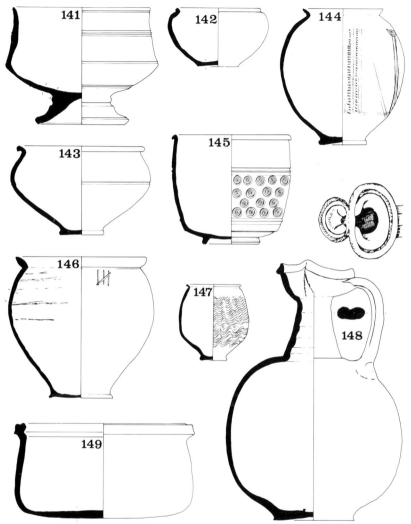

Figure V. FIRST- AND SECOND-CENTURY LOCAL WARES. Scale ¼.
141. Savernake ware pedestalled cup copying a Gallo-Belgic form; mid I.
142. Savernake ware bead-rimmed bowl; mid to late I.
143. Wattisfield ware bowl, an East Anglian regional form also recorded in Antonine Scotland; mid II (after Maynard, Brown *et al.*).
144-5. Grey or black stamped or incised imitations of samian forms, late I to early/mid II.
144. Waveney Valley ware Drag 67 beaker (after Rogerson). 145. West Stow ware Drag 30 bowl (after West).
146. Rowlands Castle cooking-jar with batch-mark; II-III (after Cunliffe).
147. Colour-coated bag-beaker, made in Wanborough area (Wiltshire); early/mid II (after Anderson).
148-9. Eburacum ware (York), late I to early II. 148. Pinch-lipped jug. 149. Bowl of form possibly introduced from North Africa (after King).

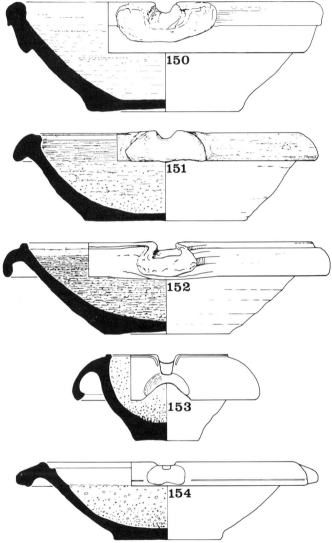

Figure VI. FIRST- AND SECOND-CENTURY MORTARIA. Scale ¼
150. Wall-sided import, probably from the Rhineland; the greyish-cream fabric, internal scoring and lack of grits are typical; 20-50 (after Niblett).
151. Flanged import from the Mayen region, Germany; gritty reddish-buff fabric, with pale grey core, sparse quartz grit and intermittent internal scoring; 30-65 (after Chadburn and Tyers).
152. Group I import from North-west France; *c.*50-80 (after Niblett/Hartley).
153. Import from the workshop of the Atisii (Aoste), Gallia Narbonensis; pink cortex, darker cream surfaces, white grits; 50-80 (after Gillam emended).
154. Raetian mortarium with lugs, probably made at Wroxeter; *c.*140-80 (after Bushe-Fox with emendations).

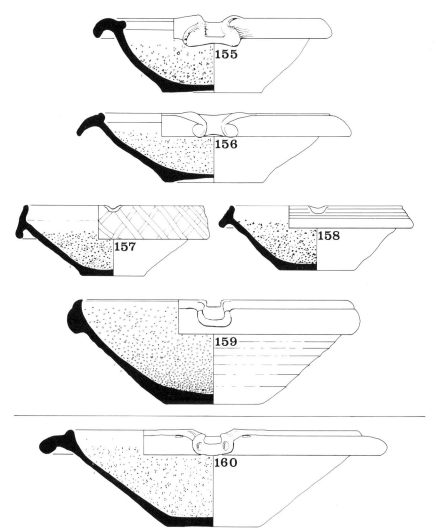

Figure VII. SECOND- TO FOURTH-CENTURY MORTARIA. Scale ¼ (except 160).
155. Rossington (Doncaster) product stamped by Sarrius, who also had a workshop at Mancetter (140-70 at Rossington; 135-70 whole career) (after Buckland/Dolby).
156-8. Mancetter/Hartshill products. 156. Mortarium with large bead rim and near-straight flange, 180-220 (after Bidwell). 157. Collared painted mortarium; 250-350. 158. Reeded hammer-head type, 250-350 (after Bidwell).
159. Imported, almost wall-sided mortarium, 160-230 (after Hanworth/Gillam).
160. Massive gritty mortarium made by Verecundus of Soller, Germany; 170-200; scale ⅛, full original diameter 76.6 cm (after Hartley, unpublished).

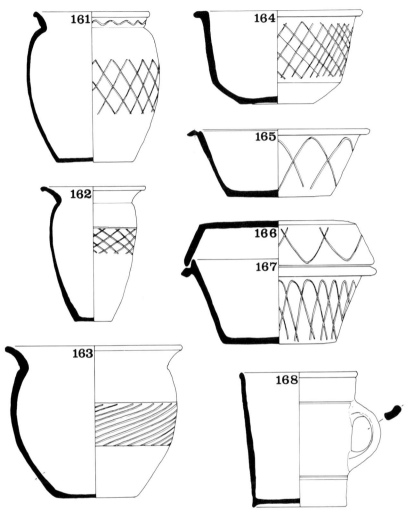

Figure VIII. BLACK-BURNISHED WARE 1 (BB1) AND SEVERN VALLEY WARE.
Scale ¼.
161. BB1 cooking-pot with acute-angled lattice; mid II (after Gillam).
162. BB1 cooking-pot with obtuse-angled lattice; mid IV (after Gillam).
163. BB1 latest local (?North Somerset) type; mid to late IV (after Leech).
164. BB1 deep chamfered bowl with flat rim; early to mid II (after Gillam).
165. BB1 bowl with incipient flange; late II to early III (after Gillam).
166. BB1 'dog-dish' used as a lid; mid IV (after Gillam).
167. BB1 bowl with developed bead-rim and flange; early IV (after Gillam).
168. Severn Valley tankard with typical basal groove; the straight (as opposed to concave)
side suggests a date in I or II (after Garrod).

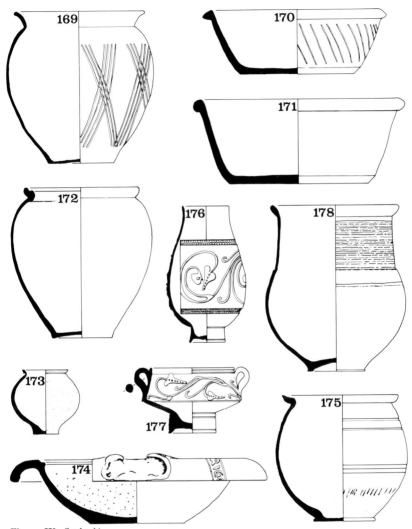

Figure IX. Scale ¼.
169-172. Black-burnished ware 2. (BB2). 169. Cooking-pot; *c.*160/90 to 260/80 (after Bidwell). 170. Bowl with pointed rim; *c.*140/50 to 185/90. 171. Bowl with beaded rim; *c.*180/90 to 240/80. 172. Thames Estuary lid-seated jar from Mucking, Essex; late II-III (after Jones).
173. South Carlton (Lincolnshire) rough-cast beaker, *c.*135-70 (after Webster).
174. South Carlton mortarium of Crico, 135-70 (after Webster).
175. Canterbury jar; a similar type (often with a reeded rim) was also made by the Verulamium region industry; *c.*120-70/80 (after Jenkins).
176-7. Central Gaulish 'rhenish ware' (black samian), mid/late II to early III. 176. Beaker; the dotted spine of the barbotine leaf is typical of this source (after Wenham). 177. Cup with 'bung-foot' (after Greene).
178. North Gaulish grey-ware *'vase troconique'*, early III (after Ellison).

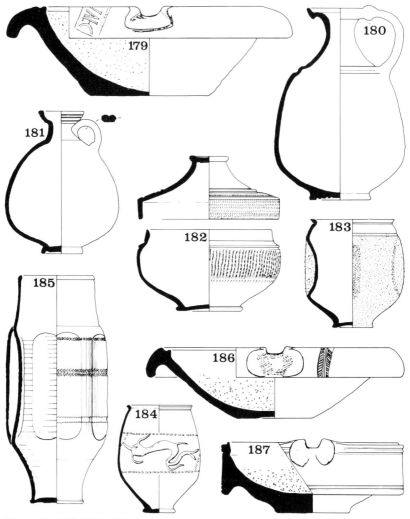

Figure X. COLCHESTER PRODUCTS. Scale ¼.
179. Mortarium made by Roman citizen potters, the Sexti Valerii; their flanges are sometimes gritted and scored; *c*.55-90+ (after Round).
180. Mica-dusted flagon imitating metal prototype; mid/late II (after Hull).
181. Ring-neck flagon with cupped mouth and uneven rings; mid II (after Hull).

182-5. Colour-coated wares. 182. Castor box; mid II-III. 183. Rough-cast beaker with cornice rim; *c*.135-80 (both after Hull). 184. Beaker with barbotine dolphin; *c*.190-230 (after Partridge). 185. Tall indented beaker, probably one of Colchester's latest colour-coated forms; *c*.230/50-70 (after Andrews).
186. Flanged herringbone-stamped mortarium, *c*.140-75 (after Hull).
187. Elaborately grooved wall-sided mortarium, a form probably introduced to Colchester by samian potters from East Gaul; *c*.160-220 (after Hull).

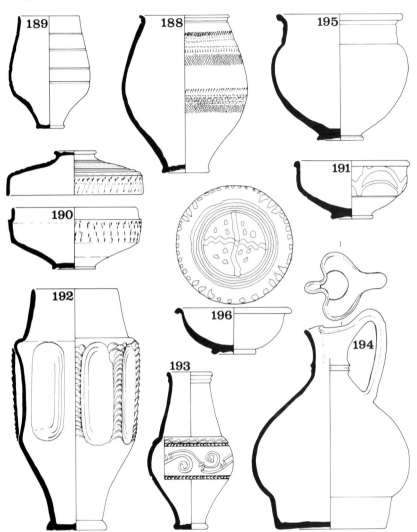

Figure XI. LOWER NENE VALLEY PRODUCTS. Scale ¼.
188-94. Colour-coated wares. 188. Rouletted cornice-rimmed beaker; late II to early III (after Perrin). 189. Grooved beaker with more angular profile; mid III (after Perrin). 190. Castor box; late II to early III (after Hadman/Upex/Wild). 191. Bowl with white painted arcs; IV (after Perrin). 192. Funnel-mouthed beaker with applied scales; mid to late III (after Andrews). 193. Globular beaker with pentice-moulding on shoulder, white painted scrolls and late rim form; probably early/mid IV (after Johnson). 194. Jug with 'drum-base'; IV, possibly first half (after Perrin). 195. Grey-ware jar of local type; late II/III (after Perrin). 196. Parchment ware bowl with brownish painted decoration; IV (after Perrin).

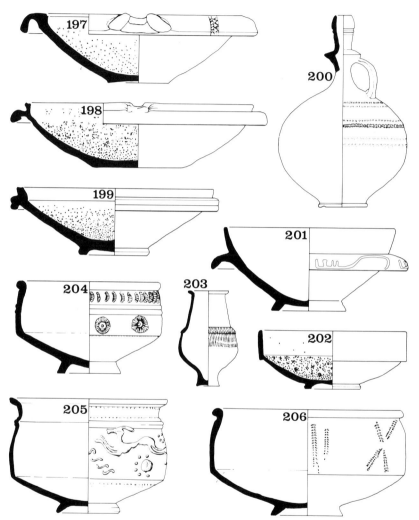

Figure XII. OXFORDSHIRE PRODUCTS AND PEVENSEY WARE. Scale ¼.
197-8. Oxfordshire white ware mortaria. 197. Early form with trade-stamp, *c.*120-60 (after Young). 198. Later type; *c.*240-300 (after Parrington).
199-205. Oxfordshire red and brown colour-coated wares. 199. Mortarium with prominent bead-rim and angular flange typical of *c.*300-400. 200. Flanged-neck flagon, *c.*240-400+. 201. Bowl imitating samian form Drag 38 with white painted scrolls; *c.*350-400+. 202. Wall-sided mortarium imitating samian form Drag 45; *c.*240-400+. 203. Miniature pentice-moulded beaker; *c.*270-400+. 204. Bowl with impressed rosettes and demi-rosettes; *c.*350-400+ (all after Young). 205. Elaborate bowl form with barbotine hunting scene; *c.*340-60 (after Keeley).
206. Wedge-stamped Pevensey ware bowl; *c.*325-400+ (after Fulford).

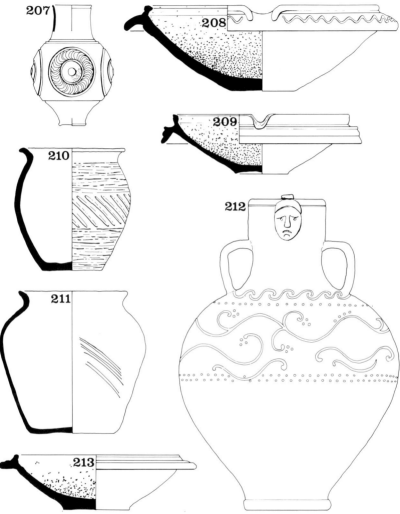

Figure XIII. MID THIRD- TO FOURTH-CENTURY PRODUCTS. Scale ¼.
207-9. New Forest wares. 207. Colour-coated beaker with incised and painted medallions; late III to early IV. 208. 'Parchment ware' mortarium with simple flange; *c*.250/60-330/40. 209. Colour-coated mortarium with angular reeded flange typical of *c*.345-90.
210. Wessex grog-tempered jar; its squat proportions and inclined burnishing may imitate the latest BB1 (figure VIII, 163); mid/late IV to early V (after Clarke).
211. Kent grog-tempered jar; end of III to early/mid V (after Jenkins).
212. Swanpool colour-coated two-handled face-neck flagon or jar (*lagena*) with white painted decoration; mid/late IV to early V (after May).
213. Swanpool mortarium with reeded flange; IV+ (after Webster and Booth).

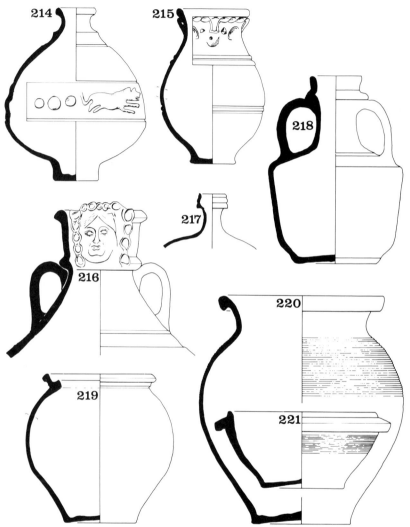

Figure XIV. HADHAM, SHELL-TEMPERED AND LATE IMPORTED WARES.
Scale ¼.

214-7. Hadham red colour-coated ware, end of III to early V. 214. Flask with barbotine
?lions and 'Romano-Saxon' style bosses; early/mid IV+. 215. Face-jar with characteristic
frilled rim; early/mid IV+. 216. Upper part of face-neck flagon with typically late
'coal-scuttle' profile; mid to late IV+ (all after Johnson). 217. Upper part of bottle-like
flask of type made in the Barley Hill Hadham kilns (after Draper).
218. German late marbled ware flagon with typical angular body (after May).
219. Mayen ware lid-seated jar; late III-IV (after Bushe-Fox).
220-1. Midland shell-gritted wares with rilled zones; late III to early V. 220. Cooking-jar
with typical undercut rim, from Gadebridge, Hertfordshire (after Neal). 221. Flanged
bowl from Great Casterton, Leicestershire (after Corder/Gillam).

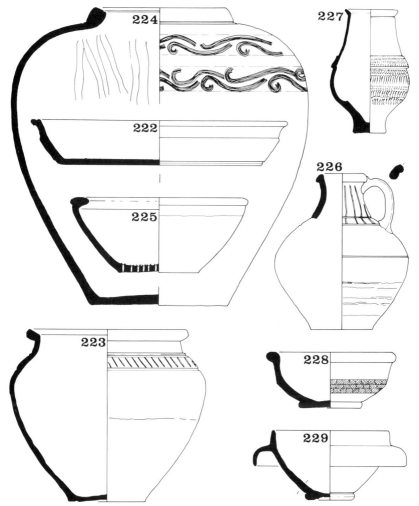

Figure XV. ALICE HOLT/FARNHAM, MESSINGHAM AND LATE IMPORTED
WARES. Scale ¼.
222-6. Alice Holt grey wares. 222. 'Atrebatic' or 'Surrey' dish, a regional type concentrated
in Surrey and adjacent areas from mid I to *c*.100. 223. Cordoned bowl; mid I to early II.
224. Large square-rimmed storage-jar with slipped zones separated by combed decoration; IV+. 225. Colander copying Mayen bowl form; end of III to early V. 226. Flagon
with 'drooping bead-rim', a type common in southern England in late III to IV+ (all after
Lyne/Jefferies).
227. Messingham (Lincolnshire) buff beaker with thickened pentice shoulder copying a
colour-coated type; first half of IV (after Rigby/Stead).
228. Argonne ware roller-stamped bowl; late III to IV (after Bushe-Fox).
229. French late marbled ware (*céramique à l'éponge*) bowl (after Cotton).

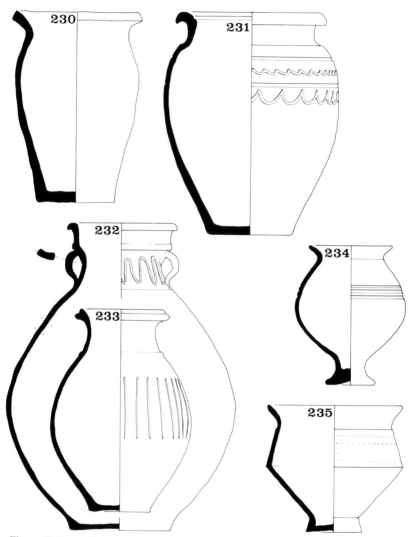

Figure XVI. EAST YORKSHIRE WARES. Scale ¼.
230-1. Handmade vessels in native calcite mineral-gritted fabric. 230. Knapton cooking-pot; mid/late I to late III (after Corder). 231. Huntcliffe-type cooking pot with wheel-finished rim and incised decoration; mid IV to early V (after Hull).
232-5. Grey burnished wares exported to the northern frontier from East Yorkshire kilns. 232. Double-handled jar or flagon; late III to mid IV. 233. Narrow-mouthed ovoid flanged jar (also made with beaded rim); mid/late III to mid IV (both after Stead/Rigby). 234. Beaker with everted rim and pedestal-foot; mid/late III to mid IV (after Bidwell). 235. Carinated bowl with pedestal-foot, from Hasholme kilns; late III to mid IV (after Hicks and Wilson).

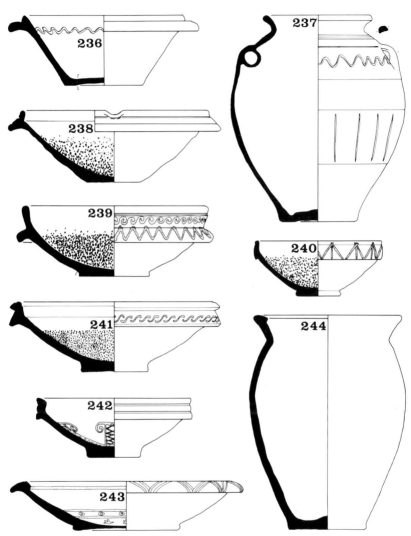

Figure XVII. CRAMBECK WARES AND DALES WARE. Scale ¼.
236-7. Crambeck grey burnished ware. 236. Flanged bowl; the internal burnished wavy line is common after *c*.360/70 (after Corder). 237. Cooking-pot with countersunk handles, developed from a native prototype with protruding looped handles; late III/early IV to 400+ (after Stead/Rigby).
238. Early Crambeck mortarium; this and allied early forms (with hammer-head, reeded or plain flange) often had a coarser cream fabric and ill-sorted grits; *c*.290-360.
239-43. Crambeck fine cream painted parchment wares, all c.360/70-400+. 239. Flanged mortarium (after Perrin). 240. Wall-sided mortarium. 241. Mortarium with 'beaked' profile (after Corder). 242. Bowl with reeded wall-side (after Hull). 243. Shallow bowl (after Corder/Hull).
244. Dales ware cooking-pot; late II to mid IV (after Wenham).

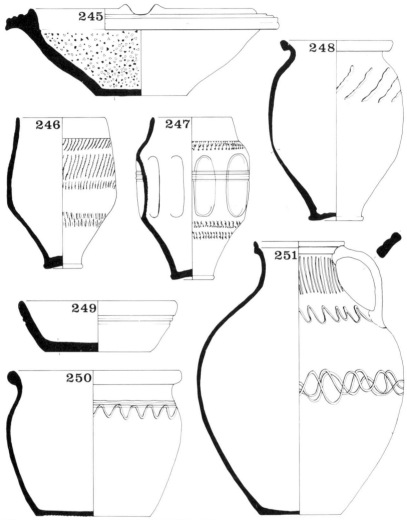

Figure XVIII. LOCAL WARES OF THE THIRD AND FOURTH CENTURIES. Scale ¼.

245-7. Pakenham wares, Suffolk (after Smedley/Owles). 245. Buff mortarium with a reeded flange, a typical East Anglian form perhaps influenced by Nene Valley products; probably mid III+. 246. Colour-coated rouletted beaker; early/mid III. 247. Colour-coated indented beaker; early/mid III.

248-9. Nar Valley ware from Shouldham kilns (Norfolk). 248. Icenian rusticated ware jar; end of II to early IV. 249. Dish copying a late black-burnished ware type; multiple grooves were a particularly common trait in East Anglian late regional pottery types; end of II to early IV.

250. Rettendon ware S-shaped cooking-jar or bowl; *c.*280/300 to 350 (after Tildesley).
251. Congresbury ware flagon; the slightly flanged rim, sometimes lid-seated as here, is typical of this industry; late III to late IV (after Rahtz).

Index

Page numbers in italic refer to illustrations